Modern Italy: A Very Short Introduction

VERY SHORT INTRODUCTIONS are for anyone wanting a stimulating and accessible way into a new subject. They are written by experts, and have been translated into more than 40 different languages.

The series began in 1995, and now covers a wide variety of topics in every discipline. The VSI library now contains over 450 volumes—a Very Short Introduction to everything from Psychology and Philosophy of Science to American History and Relativity—and continues to grow in every subject area.

Very Short Introductions available now:

Available soon:

For more information visit our website

www.oup.com/vsi/

Anna Cento Bull

MODERN ITALY

A Very Short Introduction

OXFORD
UNIVERSITY PRESS

OXFORD

UNIVERSITY PRESS

Great Clarendon Street, Oxford, OX2 6DP,
United Kingdom

Oxford University Press is a department of the University of Oxford.
It furthers the University's objective of excellence in research, scholarship,
and education by publishing worldwide. Oxford is a registered trade mark of
Oxford University Press in the UK and in certain other countries

Published in the United States of America by Oxford University Press
198 Madison Avenue, New York, NY 10016, United States of America

British Library Cataloguing in Publication Data
Data available

Library of Congress Control Number: 2016942458

ISBN 978-0-19-872651-7

Printed in Great Britain by
Ashford Colour Press Ltd, Gosport, Hampshire

Contents

Acknowledgements

Several years of teaching 'Modern and Contemporary Italy' to first-year students of Italian and witnessing their eager curiosity convinced me to undertake this project. I also relished the prospect of reading widely on areas of Italian culture which I had previously little explored. As well as reading, I asked numerous people to share their expert knowledge with me: they are too many to name but I wish to thank them all collectively for their time and patience. My academic books are not renowned for their easy accessibility and for this reason I would like to thank all those friends and family members who read my manuscript with a view to ensuring it was fully readable: David Bull, Jeremy Bull, Nicholas and Valerie Drew, Ruth Gairns, Stuart Redman, and Stephanie Tuckett. I also wish to thank the anonymous readers for their exacting and extremely helpful comments and the Oxford University Press team who helped me all the way to completion, especially Andrea Keegan and Jenny Nugee.

List of illustrations

The publisher and the author apologize for any errors or omission in the above list. If contacted they will be pleased to rectify these at the earliest opportunity.

Modern Italy

1. A map of Italy with the regions and their capitals.

Introduction

The early 21st century has proved to be a difficult time for Italy. The country has retained a wide international appeal for its heritage and culture, yet it has generally been considered in decline, seemingly struggling to regain lost ground following several years of economic crisis and political instability. In the last two decades various explanations have been put forward for this loss of dynamism, and a series of remedies have been attempted by successive governments, with uneven impact.

So what is wrong with today's Italy and why has it shown a persistent reluctance to change? How does the country currently view itself and how is it viewed from the outside? A series of unrelated events which put Italy in the international spotlight in 2014 proved to be very revealing, as they appeared to raise similar issues and concerns, even while celebrating Italian creativity. A common theme underpinning these events was a warning that the country can no longer rely on its celebrated cultural charm to make up for the deficiencies in its political institutions or economic set-up.

The first celebratory event was the award in March of an Oscar for best foreign-language film to Paolo Sorrentino's *La grande bellezza* ('The Great Beauty'), fifteen years after Benigni won it with his film, *Life is Beautiful*. As widely noted, Sorrentino's film was an obvious tribute to Fellini's *La dolce vita* (1960), the film that had depicted Rome as a place of glamour and a privileged destination for Hollywood stars. Indeed, Rome itself had become synonymous with the Italian 'sweet' way of life, marking the start of a glorious decade for Italian fashion, industry, and exports. Yet, while on the surface putting Rome once again at the centre of a flamboyant and hedonistic lifestyle, *La grande bellezza* views it through grotesque and distorted lenses, contrasting the classical beauty of the city with the senseless decadence of its current inhabitants. And whereas the protagonist of *La dolce vita*, Marcello, is a journalist dissatisfied with his own life and modern life generally, he is nevertheless young enough to be able to change course and turn to serious writing if he can find the inner resources to do so. By contrast, the protagonist of *La grande bellezza*, Jep, is an old, childless man who can only look back with regret at his wasted potential as a serious writer. Thus Sorrentino's film presents a pessimistic and gloomy view of what Italy has become, not least under the influence of what he himself defined as Berlusconi's 'culture of escapism'. At best it could be seen as a last wake-up call for intellectuals and politicians alike.

The second event worth recalling was an exhibition on 'The Glamour of Italian Fashion 1945–2014', held at the Victoria and Albert Museum in London between 5 April and 27 July 2014. Sponsored by the jeweller Bulgari and widely reviewed worldwide, the exhibition covered a large time span, ostensibly celebrating Italy's extraordinary longevity at the forefront of the fashion industry. In spite of this, most of its artefacts belonged to the golden age of the 1950s to the 1990s—and the tour concluded with filmed interviews with Italian designers who lamented the lack of support for the industry in terms of fiscal and industrial policy as well as the ageing profile of its protagonists. The exhibition curator, Sonnet Stanfill, justified the inclusion of these testimonies by stating: 'The question of the future of Italian fashion is one that we need to face squarely.'

The third event of significance was an exhibition within the 2014 Venice Biennale, which ran from 7 June to 22 November. Entitled 'Monditalia', it was entirely dedicated to Italy, its history and culture, with forty-one architectural projects focusing on different subjects and covering the entire length of the peninsula. Recurrent themes revolved around immigration, the dilapidation of public spaces and buildings, and political dysfunction. Echoing the central theme of *La grande bellezza*, the Biennale Director, Dutch architect Rem Koolhaas, justified the decision to dedicate a special exhibition to Italy by defining it as a 'fundamental country' at a time of crucial political change, adding that it was 'emblematic of a global situation where...basically every country in the world struggles with this paradox: on the one hand, unbelievable gifts, on the other hand, an inability to realise them'. Seemingly to underline this paradox, the opening of 'Monditalia' was marked by a corruption scandal engulfing the mayor of Venice, the president of the Veneto region, and other prominent local politicians from the mainstream parties, including Berlusconi's centre-right party, Forza Italia, and the main centre-left party, Partito Democratico. The system of kickbacks around a publicly funded flagship barrier designed to prevent Venice from being flooded in winter was exposed just days after a similar scandal was unearthed by investigators around Expo 2015, the Milan-based world fair due to open in May 2015. Both scandals were eerily reminiscent of the 'Clean Hands' investigation that brought down the entire political system—the so-called First Republic—in the early 1990s.

The final event worth recalling was the appointment of Matteo Renzi as prime minister in February 2014. Aged 39, Renzi was the youngest prime minister in the history of Italy and a self-styled advocate of the need to send to the scrapyard (*rottamare*, hence his nickname of *rottamatore*) most of the country's ageing political establishment. Elected leader of the Partito Democratico in 2013, almost as a last resort following this party's poor electoral results, he appeared to embody a widespread thirst for radical change.

Almost on cue with the themes highlighted in the events described earlier, Renzi made a point of linking Italy's future to its cultural heritage and history, and, as when he had been mayor of Florence, he highlighted the crucial role of culture for economic recovery and of politics for sustaining both. Hence his highly symbolic personal appearances at the opening of the London fashion exhibition in April and of the Florence international fashion fair 'Pitti Uomo' in June, and his trip to China and Vietnam in June in order to 'write a new page of the Made in Italy story'.

Renzi's deliberate adoption of the 'Made in Italy' brand to herald a return to the country's halcyon days and promote a second 'economic miracle' marked an attempt to re-establish a convincing and bold narrative on Italy's future, revolving around innovation, modernization, and rejuvenation. It came after a period in which the failure of Berlusconi's promise to bring material well-being appeared to indicate that Italians were no longer reconciled to the project of modernity. The critique of modernity is not just an academic exercise as far as Italy is concerned. This disaffection has spurred sustained opposition to grandiose public works projects like the long-standing movement against the construction of a high-speed railway line in the Susa Valley near Turin or indeed the campaign against the much-touted bridge linking Sicily to the mainland. It is no coincidence that in 1989 Italy spearheaded the international Slow Food movement whose manifesto proclaimed that 'In the name of productivity, the "fast life" has changed our lifestyle and now threatens our environment and our land (and city) scapes'.

One of the arguments that this volume will put forward is that Italy has experienced great difficulty, since its inception as a nation-state, in developing and putting across, both domestically and externally, a convincing story of what it means to be Italian and what Italy stands for. All nation-states are characterized by the presence of diverse and often contradictory narratives but at different times in their history some of these narratives succeed in simultaneously defining and driving forward the nation's 'mission'. In the Italian case, the existence of competing visions has often been a source of dynamism and innovation, but it has also resulted in deep internal divisions and strife—even civil war. Indeed, one influential reading of modern Italian history sees the country as having been in the grip of a never-ending albeit low-intensity civil war, which from time to time erupts into open conflict.

In this reading, modern Italy has not really changed since Dante's times, when the two rival factions of the pro-papacy Guelfs and the pro-empire Ghibellines fought each other and alternately gained control of the government of major cities. This constant strife led many communes to replace their republican institutions with a single ruler called from outside the city (the *Podestà*) who would be entrusted with full powers in order to put an end to political divisions and violence. Perhaps unsurprisingly, a recent interpretation of the Italian technocratic (i.e. expert and non-political) government headed by Mario Monti and lasting from December 2011 to April 2012 referred to him as a modern-day *Podestà* (Di Virgilio and Radaelli 2013). In his capacity as a former EU commissioner standing outside of party politics, he was entrusted with the re-establishment of Italy's credibility abroad and with overcoming political divisions at home.

Nowhere was the existence of competing and mutually exclusive narratives as much in evidence as in 2011 when Italy celebrated 150 years of unification. It proved to be a difficult and controversial anniversary, for various reasons. The northern-based, separatist Northern League party, despite being in government as part of the right-wing, Berlusconi-led coalition and thus co-responsible for organizing the official commemorative events, openly threatened to boycott the celebrations. Indeed 17 March, the day in 1861 which saw the proclamation of the unified Italian kingdom under Victor Emmanuel II, was dubbed by Northern League MPs a 'day of mourning'. Political divisions were exacerbated by the controversial figure of Prime Minister Silvio Berlusconi, who by then was facing charges of abuse of office, which were soon to be followed by two no-confidence motions in Parliament. The country was about to enter another prolonged cycle of recession, causing the 'spread' (i.e. the difference between each country on how much they paid in interest rates) between Italy and Germany to reach an unprecedented level later in the year, ultimately causing the downfall of the Berlusconi government and a new period of political instability.

Against this backdrop a number of intellectuals and commentators openly questioned Italy's achievements since its unification, casting gloomy predictions on its continuing viability and even survival. Yet, contrary to all expectations, the celebrations attracted popular support and provided a moment of national unity, with only 21 per cent of Italians, according to a reputable opinion poll, declaring themselves 'indifferent' to the anniversary. Furthermore, 88 per cent of Italians and even 70 per cent of League voters stated that unification had been a good thing for the country.

In many ways the disputes surrounding the 150th anniversary since the Unification epitomize long-standing debates on 'modern' (post-Unification) Italy, and go to the very heart of what we understand as 'modernity'. On the one hand, Italy had for some time been depicted as a deeply divided, failed nation-state, which had proved unable to modernize itself fully or to overcome its structural weaknesses. Modernity in this case is viewed as an unrealized ideal and a perennially incomplete economic, social, and political project. At the economic level, the country is often deemed to have relied upon a hopelessly inward-looking and fragile model of development based on small family firms in the North and on a state-dependent model of inflated public sector employment in the South. At the social level, these interpretations have revolved around the persisting gap between the North and the South in terms of standards of living and employment rates, the resilience of organized crime like the Sicilian Mafia and the Neapolitan Camorra, and a widespread mentality known as 'amoral familism' which places the interests of kin and friends before the public good. At the political level, the emphasis has been on the twisted nature of Italian democracy where the relationship between voters and parties is characterized by patron–client ties and nepotism, and where the political class is deeply divided in ideological terms but united by corruption and self-interest.

On the other hand, a relatively recent 'revisionist' strand of interpretation contests the traditional vision of the peninsula at the time of unification as defined by economic, social, and political backwardness, and places its development since then fully in the context of European and global modernizing trends. Far from being an 'exceptional' case of failed nationhood and persistent traditional traits, Italy is deemed to be on a par with other nation-states. Despite lacking natural resources and having limited arable land, the country was able to develop a large manufacturing and services sector, and in the 1980s had become the fifth largest industrial power in the world. Although it has subsequently slipped a few places, it is currently part of the group of eight leading industrialized nations (G8). Despite the continuing influence of the Catholic Church, Italy introduced divorce in 1974 and legalized abortion in 1978; it also ranks as one of the developed countries with the lowest fertility rate (1.4 in 2011, on a par with Germany and Japan) and one of the highest life expectancies (ahead of France, Germany, Sweden, the UK, and the USA in 2013). In the last two decades it has attracted a large number of migrants who today make up more than 8 per cent of the population, characterizing Italy as *de facto* multicultural, along with most European countries, even though it is experiencing some difficulty in coming to terms with this profound change. In short, while the country has been experiencing a prolonged recession in recent years and may even be on a declining path in terms of its competitiveness, it would be wrong to view its trajectory since Unification solely from the perspective of this negative trend.

This short book explores the country's difficulties in developing and disseminating a strong and credible national vision for a domestic and international audience while also examining its extraordinary ability to seduce the world thanks to the 'soft' power of its culture and the 'Made in Italy' brand. It argues that its political class—with the exception of those of the fascist period—has tended to overcome internal divisions through ruling by consensus and relying on economic growth and prosperity to bind Italians together, which explains its current predicament. Finally, it probes the extent to which modernity still represents a shared vision among Italian intellectuals, political leaders, and ordinary people.

Chapter 1
Modernity and resurgence in the making of Italy

The history of modern Italy has been characterized by recurrent cultural and political projects of modernity, rejuvenation, and regeneration. The Risorgimento ('Resurgence'), the movement leading to the Italian Unification in 1861, explicitly linked the quest for national unity to a process of moral regeneration and progress. Later forms of nationalism and the rise of fascism in the first two decades of the 20th century advocated a spiritual revolution and the moulding of new Italians through war and violence as the only means of creating a modernized but also spiritually reborn nation that would be at the forefront of a new European civilization.

Italy's successive projects of modernity have often had at their roots a profound dissatisfaction with its social and political reality as well as with perceived moral values and national traits, representing these in negative terms. Hence the theme of 'resurgence' has been inextricably linked to that of 'decadence' and the theme of 'national purification' to those of 'corruption' and 'degeneration'. Comparisons with Europe (northern Europe in particular) have also played an important role, with Italian (and non-Italian) intellectuals often painting a picture of a society constantly needing to 'catch up' with and not be left behind by the rest of Europe. From the perspective of many intellectual and political movements, modernization could only be achieved through a process of emulation of the other nations' achievements accompanied by a reworking of glorious national traditions (especially those linked to the myth of ancient Rome).

It is possible to envisage the history of modern Italy as unfolding in cycles: starting with the Unification, when a 'resurgence from decadence' was advocated and brought to the forefront, followed by a period in which the political class focused on addressing socio-economic issues through mediation and compromise, which in turn created a sense of unfulfilled expectations. Another attempt at moral resurgence was made by Prime Minister Francesco Crispi, mainly through the pursuit of colonial wars in the period 1887–96. Italy's defeat at the hands of Ethiopia in 1896 (the most humiliating defeat for a European power on African soil) put paid to that attempt. This was followed by Italy's 'Belle Epoque', when Giovanni Giolitti (1903–14) again focused on achieving consensus through political mediation and compromise as well as through raising living standards. At the beginning of the new century, his vision of Italy (dubbed *Italietta* or 'Little Italy') was increasingly spurned by intellectuals. Instead they launched a grand vision of a heroic and glorious 'Great Italy', a project which required a 'New Resurgence' from decadence and which eventually led to the collapse of liberal Italy and to a fascist dictatorship. At the end of the fascist period (1943–5), when Italy was torn apart by a bloody war between fascists and anti-fascists, the myth of a 'New Resurgence' was taken on by the (mainly communist) Partisans. It is only after 1945 with the dominance of Christian democracy that the theme of resurgence became detached from aggressive forms of nationalism bent on war-making, and was made to coincide with the project of European integration.

It is also possible to argue that each of the cycles outlined above has a common characteristic pointing to an unresolved issue in modern and contemporary Italy: a huge chasm between generations whereby each new generation feels excluded, even oppressed, by the previous one and rebels against it. The

Risorgimento was undoubtedly marked by a very high level of participation and enthusiasm on the part of young people, who felt invested with the task of building a glorious future out of a sclerotic present. The widespread disappointment with Giolitti's 'Little Italy' was memorably portrayed in a book by Luigi Pirandello published in 1909 and significantly entitled *I vecchi e i giovani* ('The Young and the Old') as a divide between an older generation, mired in corruption and therefore responsible for betraying the hopes of the Risorgimento, and a young generation, left feeling oppressed. The fascist movement not only appealed to many young people, entrusting them with the mission of restoring pre-eminence to their homeland, but also turned youth itself into a powerful symbol of national renewal and regeneration. The youth rebellion of 1968–9, while being part of a European-wide phenomenon, degenerated in Italy into bloody violence carried out by groups of young people against a 'system' perceived as immobile and impervious to their needs and demands. The Italy of today notoriously has a youth problem because the young carry a disproportionate burden from the country's economic crisis—at least in terms of unemployment and future prospects.

It seems paradoxical that a country in which family ties have always been strong, playing a crucial role in cementing social cohesion, seems unable to ensure an unproblematic transition from one generation to the next. Yet it is possibly the very safeguarding of strong family ties, in both legal and cultural terms, that skews the balance of power in favour of the parents' generation and contributes to a sense of impotence and feelings of rebellion among the young, at least until they themselves are able to replace their predecessors (thus renewing the cycle). It is also the case, however, that each generation, as well as rebelling against the old, tends to be cross-cut by deep internal divisions, often of an ideological nature. This situation prevents the emergence of unifying narratives, and can have a paralysing effect in terms of the exercising of cultural and political power within the country. It may also lead to one or more sides viewing their fellow nationals as 'sworn enemies' thereby justifying their having recourse to violence in order to impose their vision of society upon the nation as a whole.

The Risorgimento: moral resurgence after decadence

The patriots of the Risorgimento were convinced that divided Italy had fallen into a state of decline and backwardness vis-à-vis the major (northern) European powers since the heyday of the Renaissance. They felt the country was in need of a moral and cultural 'resurgence' in order to gain its place among modern nation-states. The political division of the country was clearly perceived as the main cause of Italy's state of decadence, but also an incapacity to overcome traditionally weak national traits. Hence the Italian nation needed to be forged through blood and sacrifice, and (male) Italians had to be able to demonstrate strength, virility, and military prowess. Women were to lend their support in ways that would not put into question their own traditional family roles. A subordinate narrative pitted the North of the country against the South, attributing to the former, judged to be the more advanced area, the mission of bringing civilization to the latter, rescuing it from bad government and 'feudal' practices. In short, they felt that if the Unification was to succeed in bringing Italy closer to northern Europe, the process would have to be overseen by Italy's North, this being the area of the country closest to the ideal to which the movement aspired.

The Risorgimento has traditionally been viewed as a minority movement incapable of exercising moral and cultural dominance, and dependent upon foreign powers for its success. The Italian communist thinker Antonio Gramsci famously called it a 'passive revolution' with reference to the lack of mobilization of the peasant masses on the part of the nationalist elites. More recently, the movement has been revisited by both Italian and non-Italian historians, who have positively recognized its capacity to penetrate and galvanize large sectors of Italian society. This, it is argued, was achieved through the mass appeal of charismatic figures like Giuseppe Garibaldi; the martyrdom of many young fighters ready to volunteer and die in the name of their nation; and the works of creative artists in the fields of literature, poetry, and opera. Giuseppe Verdi's operas, in particular, can often be (and were at the time) interpreted as being supportive of national patriotism. Most famously *Nabucco* (1842), which focused on the plight of the Jews during their captivity in Babylon, contains the well-known chorus of the Hebrew slaves, 'Va pensiero'—almost a second national anthem for Italy. Opera houses were important public meeting places in numerous Italian cities and towns, and, especially in those parts of northern and central Italy under Austrian rule, were able to express political dissent through both the music and the audiences' enthusiastic reaction to it.

This is not to say that all patriots agreed on their vision of the future or on how to achieve their goals. Indeed they were deeply divided between those, like Giuseppe Mazzini, who favoured a revolutionary-insurrectionary path to liberation from foreign rule and the unification of the peninsula into a republican State (the so-called 'democrats') and those, like Camillo Benso, Count of Cavour, who was prime minister of Piedmont from 1852 onwards, who viewed popular insurrection as anathema. These so-called 'moderates' gradually came to see the creation of a (northern) monarchical State through the leadership of the Kingdom of Piedmont-Sardinia and the deployment of its regular army as the best way forward.

Cavour's steadfast adherence to a liberal constitution after the failure of the 1848 revolutions, at a time when the other States in the peninsula hurried to repeal the ones they had conceded under pressure from the insurgents, allowed Piedmont to emerge as a beacon of freedom and the rule of law—an example of a modern liberal-parliamentary State. This gained it a leading role in the process of unification, yet the peninsula would not have come together into a single nation-state without Garibaldi's famous 'Expedition of the Thousand' to Sicily, from where he promoted a bottom-up insurrection against Bourbon rule, which led him to enter Naples as victor only to then hand over control to the Piedmontese king. While the attitude of European powers, not least Britain, played an important role in allowing the expedition to succeed, its success nevertheless re-established the credentials and validity of the revolutionary path in the eyes of the democrats and became part of the national mythology. In 1861 the new kingdom of Italy was officially established, even though Venice and Rome were not part of it. Venice was annexed in 1866 (thanks to Italy's alliance with Prussia against Austria and despite a disastrous military campaign) and Rome in 1871 (following its capture on 20 September 1870 when the Italian troops entered the city by force).

In the face of the extraordinary success that was the unification of the country (William Gladstone called it 'a marvel' and 'one of the great events of the century') and the lofty ideals and redemptory role it had been invested with, it should come as no surprise that the period which followed fell well short of people's expectations and represented an abrupt return to reality. Two issues that were to have a deep and long-standing impact on the history of modern Italy up to the present day came to the fore immediately after the Unification and contrasted head on with both the triumphalist dominant narrative and the myth of moral resurgence. The first was the rift between the new liberal State and the Catholic Church, with the latter condemning liberalism as an evil doctrine and becoming a fierce critic of the Italian nation-state. In a country in which the vast majority of the population were practising Catholics, the intransigent opposition of the Catholic Church and the Pope's decision in 1868 (known as the *Non Expedit*) to forbid all Catholics from taking part in politics, either as voters or as candidates, created a deep fault-line and above all deprived the newly formed nation-state of an important source of moral legitimacy.

The second issue was the widespread peasant rebellion in Italy's South, which was put down by the use of (arguably excessive) force by the State, afraid of its consequences in terms of national unity. Fomented by the deposed rulers and degraded in status by being labelled 'great brigandage', it was in fact an expression of widespread social unrest which had its roots in the desperate conditions of the peasantry. It also demonstrated the imperviousness of this social group to the rhetoric of national patriotism (and also to an extent the partial validity of Gramsci's thesis of a 'passive revolution'). The brutality with which the rebellion was put down in the name of restoring order to a lawless society left some deep scars which have since been a source of anti-Risorgimento themes.

The rebellion put into stark relief what was to become known as the 'Southern Question', giving rise to numerous representations of the South by intellectuals and creative artists. In many cases, intellectuals, including those from the South, upheld the idea that this part of the country was plagued by a series of ills of an economic, social, political, and above all cultural nature, which retarded its development compared with the North. However, a few prominent southern writers expressed disillusionment with the very ideals of progress and modernity linked to the Risorgimento.

The Sicilian writer Giovanni Verga, in particular, was critical of the impact of modernity brought by the Unification upon the island in his famous 1881 novel *I Malavoglia* ('The House of the Medlar Tree'). He depicts the fishing village of Aci Trezza as a community bewildered, disrupted, and, in the case of the Malavoglia family itself, ultimately ruined by both external developments and corrosive new values, especially the quest for individual affirmation and material wealth. As the author stated in the preface, he was interested in the plight of those who were defeated 'whom the current [of progress] has strewn along the banks'. A year later, in 1882, Verga published a short story,

'La libertà' ('Freedom'), based on a true episode, the repression of a peasant uprising in the small Sicilian town of Bronte by Garibaldi's second-in-command, Nino Bixio. The story offers a pessimistic vision of the Expedition of the Thousand, as it revolves around the differing interpretations of the ideals of freedom, justice, and progress, which the insurgents interpret as represented by a fair distribution of the land ('Freedom meant that everybody should have their share') while the Garibaldini feel it incumbent upon themselves to uphold the rule of law.

As a result, a sense of moral resurgence and nationhood appeared to many to remain elusive. Some looked to economic development and/or children's education as a means of creating a sense of Italian identity. While successive governments introduced and then extended compulsory primary education, children's literature aimed at instilling a new morality. The famous story of *Pinocchio*, first serialized by Carlo Collodi in 1880, was primarily an allegory of the coming of age of Italy—from being a puppet manipulated and controlled by others it developed into an independent and responsible being. It was also a morality tale about how Italians—not only children—should behave: work hard rather than expect handouts or miracles; take care of one's elders; value education. The much more sentimental *Cuore* ('Heart'), serialized by Edmondo De Amicis in 1886, comprised several short stories revolving around children's idealized behaviour, aimed at teaching younger generations civic and patriotic virtues: love of their country; respect for authority; the spirit of sacrifice; heroism; charity; piety; obedience; and endurance of hardship.

Whether these educational projects succeeded in instilling a sense of patriotism among the less educated classes is a moot point. Indeed, in the 1870s and 1880s, the lower classes seemed more attracted to radical revolutionary ideologies than to patriotism. In the 1870s and 1880s anarchism spread through the countryside, inspired by the ideas of the Russian exile, Mikhail Bakunin, who believed in overthrowing the established system through peasant revolts and even terrorist means—dramatically demonstrated in 1900 when the Italian king, Humbert I, was murdered by Italian-American anarchist Gaetano Bresci. The most influential and enduring ideology among the working classes, however, was that of socialism. Established in the early 1890s it soon developed into two strands, one reformist and the other revolutionary. The former strand was favourable to reaching an understanding with Prime Minister Giolitti while the latter was bent on taking over power by insurrectionary means.

Fear of socialism led Pope Leo XIII (1878–1903) to relax the *Non Expedit* ruling: Catholics started to vote and, at local elections, they were even allowed to stand as candidates. The same pope also took a stance in relation to the social question, publishing the encyclical *Rerum Novarum* (1891), which denounced the capitalist exploitation of workers ('The misery and wretchedness pressing so unjustly on the majority of the working class') while condemning the doctrine of socialism. In 1904–5 his successor, Pope Pius X (1903–14), opted for an agreement with conservative liberals who professed to hold Catholic values. In parallel with these initiatives, between 1870 and 1912, the Church supported thousands of social associations, grouped into a body called Catholic Action in the new century.

The rise and spread of these new movements, coupled with Giolitti's strategy aimed at integrating them into liberal-parliamentary politics, not least through recourse to constant bargaining and even corrupt deals, contributed to a growing discrediting of his political leadership among intellectuals and to the elaboration of a new aggressive project of modernity among some of them.

Modernity through war

At the beginning of the 20th century, the propulsive force of the Risorgimento as a project of modernity came to an end. It had lost the ability to achieve poignant and emotional resonance among the new generation, especially as those who had played a direct role in unifying the country became elderly or died. Indeed, as discussed earlier, the Sicilian writer, Luigi Pirandello, accused the older generation of having betrayed the ideals of the Risorgimento. It was primarily a group of avant-garde Florentine intellectuals, however, who first elaborated a new and ambitious project of regeneration and modernity in the early 1900s, drawing on a theme of a 'revolt against reason' put forward by European philosophers like the French Henri Bergson and Georges Sorel.

As founders and collaborators of new cultural and literary journals (*Il Regno*: 1903–6; *La Voce*: 1908–13; *Lacerba*: 1913–15; *L'Italia futurista*: 1916–18), these intellectuals viewed Liberal Italy under Giolitti, with its emphasis on political compromise and social consensus sustained by economic development, as epitomizing decadence and mediocrity. They strongly objected to modernity, which they understood as the source of material progress and greed; the triumph of parliamentary politics (for the founder of *La Voce*, Giovanni Papini, Parliament was just a stage for comic shows); the emergence of mass societies made up of indistinct and anonymous individuals; and the quest for a comfortable lifestyle together with an uncritical acceptance of a peaceful coexistence between peoples. In its place, they advocated a radically alternative vision of modernity, where spiritual principles, human heroism, and military prowess, coupled with technological innovation, would transform 'Little Italy' into a great power able to exercise a civilizing influence on the world. Only a far-reaching cultural revolution could propel Italy into this new role: this ambitious project required, as in the case of the Risorgimento, a change in the national character, an overhaul of the moral compass of Italians, and their moulding into warriors ready to fight, since only through war could Italy take its place as one of the great modern world powers.

The glorification of war and violence and their crucial role in promoting a national renewal were central to the ideas of the

Italian artistic movement known as 'Futurism'. Its main proponent, Filippo Marinetti, famously proclaimed in the movement's 1909 manifesto that war was 'the world's only hygiene' and that beauty was to be found in speed and aggressive fighting—hence, art 'can be nothing but violence, cruelty, and injustice' (Figure 2). The same manifesto exalted (male) youth rebellion and power, proudly stating that 'the eldest amongst us are thirty years old' and advocating the completion of their mission within a decade, when they would be replaced by a younger cohort. Women were once again relegated to a subordinate role, indeed the manifesto condemned feminism—since the 1880s Italy had seen a spread of associations demanding female suffrage—and expressed 'contempt for woman'.

All these intellectuals viewed themselves as being invested with a political, rather than purely cultural, mission, and some politicians in turn drew eagerly on their ideas. The outcome was a new political movement, the Italian Nationalist Association, founded in 1910 by, among others, Enrico Corradini—an intellectual who explicitly associated war with modernity and Italy with a 'proletarian nation' needing to transform itself into a colonialist and imperial power through a revival of the spirit and values of ancient Rome. This association played an important role in convincing Giolitti that Italy should go to war against Turkey for the conquest of Libya in 1911. Following on from the success (and the popularity) of this colonial war, when the First World War broke out the nationalists rallied around the 'interventionist' cause against those who advocated neutrality (and who constituted the majority both in Parliament and in the country at large). The nationalists believed that participation in the conflict would impose a sense of identity and a strong discipline upon all Italians, which were considered prerequisites for becoming a great power.

It was then that Benito Mussolini made a spectacular U-turn, replacing his previous pro-neutrality stance with enthusiastic

2. 'Charge of the Lancers', 1915 painting by futurist artist Umberto Boccioni depicting the power and energy unleashed by war.

support for intervention in the war. An intellectual himself as well as a revolutionary socialist, Mussolini had been editor of the Socialist Party newspaper *Avanti!* from 1912, but he had been ousted in 1914 for refusing to toe the party line. In the same year he founded a newspaper whose very title—*Popolo d'Italia* ('People of Italy')—signalled his new patriotic and nationalist credentials.

Albeit a minority project, the campaign for intervening in the war orchestrated in Italy by the new movements was a highly visible and vociferous one. It finally succeeded in forcing the hand of Parliament and taking the country to war on the side of the Allies on 24 May 1915 (dubbed 'Radiant May' by the nationalists). However, the hyperbolic and heroic representations of war evoked by many creative artists and by politicians like Mussolini clashed with the harsh reality of life in the trenches and with the casualty figures—600,000 Italian soldiers were killed during the war. In the major defeat at Caporetto (Kobarid) in October–November 1917 at the hands of Austro-Hungarian and German forces, there were over 40,000 casualties, 300,000 captured, and as many again disbanded or deserting. 'Caporetto' has remained a term in the Italian language signifying a catastrophic debacle—perhaps the clearest proof of the huge gulf separating cultural images and discourses from social reality. As in the case of 'great brigandage' in the South after the Unification, it indicated starkly that a sizeable part of the Italian conscripted army did not share or understand the glorious mission intellectual avant-gardes had envisaged for it, not least since the infantry during the First World War was primarily made up of peasants, the social group with the highest level of illiteracy (around 37 per cent across Italy as a whole in 1911, and exceeding 50 per cent in the southern regions).

Yet this defeat served only to spur those who had advocated intervention in the war to make even greater efforts to change the national psyche and achieve a spiritual rebirth. Making Italy a great country through turning Italians into unswerving warriors fighting their external enemies remained a valid proposition which appeared vindicated when the army achieved an important victory at Vittorio Veneto in 1918. However, ensuring that the modernizing minority would impose its vision upon a recalcitrant majority by successfully fighting the 'enemies within'—socialists, democrats, pacifists, protesters, and strikers—took on a new significance after Caporetto and even more so in the aftermath of the war as a whole, when internal social and political divisions proved only to have been exacerbated by the conflict.

Chapter 2
Alternative projects
of nationhood

The aftermath of the First World War saw the country torn apart
by competing visions of what modern Italy should stand for and
the values that should bind Italians together. Against a background
of high inflation, high unemployment, and widespread social
protests, amid soaring trade-union membership and militancy,
liberals, Catholics, socialists, nationalists, and later fascists vied
with each other for popular support of their ideas and visions.

After an initial period when Italy seemed to be on the brink of a
socialist revolution, fascism gained the upper hand. Mussolini
founded the fascist movement in March 1919 and in October
1922 was appointed prime minister. This supremacy was not
achieved through persuasion and propaganda alone, but through
the use of fascist paramilitary violence and the suppression of the
liberal-democratic parliamentary system. In 1925-6, Mussolini
put an end to the liberal system and set up a dictatorship, bent on
achieving a radical transformation of the Italian nation.

Not surprisingly, the tragic outcome of the fascist project and the
anti-fascist resistance movement (1943-5) led to the emergence of
new visions of nationhood and modernity during the post-war
First Republic (1945-92), in which nationalist and patriotic myths
played only a marginal role, and European integration was
embraced with conviction.

The failure of a totalitarian project

Recent scholarship on Italian fascism has argued that it constituted a radical attempt to achieve cultural rebirth and has also emphasized the overall coherence of its ideology. This approach is in stark contrast to previous interpretations which viewed it as an eclectic movement bent on achieving power but lacking a clear vision. Indeed the expression 'fascist culture' was often considered a contradiction in terms. The recent perspective has highlighted the extent to which the fascist movement was 'revolutionary', albeit not in socio-economic terms, and the regime established after 1925 was alarmingly serious in striving to establish the State as a sacred entity with Mussolini as its deity as well as its 'Duce'. This also means, however, that the dictatorship should be judged against its own declared aims. Hence, whereas the regime used to be assessed according to the degree of consensus ('passive' as well as 'active') it managed to secure, the new interpretation has raised the stakes, as the question now revolves around whether it succeeded in moulding Italians into believers of the new secular religion and into warriors prepared to fight for it. The answer to this question has to be negative. Furthermore, the failure of the fascist project was only partially due to military defeat, as Mussolini himself had to acknowledge with increasing frustration.

The dictatorship strove to achieve its goal of totalitarianism through a variety of means, most notably through propaganda, persuasion, and indoctrination. It is notoriously difficult to judge reception among audiences exposed to these means, given media censorship. Also, fascism wanted to suppress all social unrest and incorporate the masses into the nation-state through regimentation, control, and, if necessary, coercion. To this end, it created mass organizations—such as trade-unions, leisure and sports associations, and paramilitary corps—where Italians could be brainwashed into accepting and interiorizing fascist goals and ideals, and through which the principles of authority and discipline would be inculcated.

On the surface, fascist organizations set up to mobilize Italians in support of the regime were highly successful, at least in terms of membership and participation. In 1936, the membership of the fascist party was over two million and that of the fascist youth organization Opera Balilla was over five and a half million. At its peak, the after-work leisure organization OND recruited roughly 40 per cent of industrial workers and 80 per cent of public and private employees. However, the level of indoctrination achieved by these organizations must be put in doubt, not least if we consider the crucial role of the family in socializing and educating the young. My own mother, who was born in 1921, has always maintained that she participated enthusiastically in fascist youth activities and particularly enjoyed singing the party anthem 'Giovinezza, Giovinezza' ('Youth, Youth') at public events. At home, however, she refrained from singing it as it was obviously disliked by her father, the political implications of which she came to understand only in later years.

Some policies attracted popular support, especially the reclamation, launched in 1928, of the Pontine Marshes near Rome and the accompanying building of new towns such as Sabaudia in a functional, modernist architectural style which symbolized fascist order and authority. The scheme lent itself to a huge propaganda campaign for creating jobs and transforming unproductive swamps into fertile land for farming families as well as for developing a modern urban landscape embodying fascist ideals. Also popular was the agreement with the Catholic Church, mending a long-standing rift with the Italian State. The Lateran Pacts—made up of a Conciliation Treaty, a Financial Convention, and a Concordat—signed on 11 February 1929 by Mussolini and by Cardinal Pietro Gasparri, secretary of state to the Vatican, were a triumph for the regime. They secured for it the endorsement and support of the Church ahead of that year's first plebiscite, held on

24 March, which saw Catholics instructed to vote 'yes' to the single fascist list standing for election to Parliament.

The results of the plebiscite were another resounding success for Mussolini, with only 10 per cent of abstentions and 98.3 per cent of the votes cast being in favour. Yet there was a price to pay on the part of the regime, especially in the form of Article 43 of the Concordat, according to which 'The Italian State recognizes the organizations dependent on the Italian Catholic action in so far as the Holy See has disposed that they carry out their activity outside any political party...for the diffusion and exercise of Catholic principles'. Clashes between Church and State soon after 1929 specifically on the issue of Catholic youth organizations testify to the growing awareness by Mussolini that here stood a major obstacle to the process of indoctrination of the Italian youth. Ostensibly charged with engaging in political activity, the Catholic organizations' real threat to the regime consisted in their doctrinal teaching, based on a rejection of the fascist project of modernity, especially as concerned the totalitarian and spiritual role attributed to the State.

After 1936 Mussolini's increasingly belligerent policies failed to meet with the enthusiasm of the population, as is well documented, despite representing an integral part of the fascist revolutionary and transformative vision of nationhood. The alliance with Hitler, started in 1936 and further cemented with the 1939 Pact of Steel, did not arouse any significant support and in fact caused much worry among the population. The racial laws against Italy's Jewish population, introduced in 1938, were not, as previously supposed, only in imitation of Nazi Germany—they were thoroughly implemented and not openly opposed, although anti-Semitism was not a major preoccupation among Italians at the time. Italian Jews only numbered roughly 47,000 and had previously been well integrated into society. The declaration of war against the Allies, on 10 June 1940, was greeted with the usual public demonstrations of enthusiastic support, but the Duce knew that the enthusiasm was not authentic. As his son-in-law Costanzo Ciano, then foreign minister, reported in his diary on 29 January 1940, Mussolini himself had by then come to realize the futility of trying to mould Italians into warriors. On that occasion, he asked rhetorically, 'Have you ever seen a lamb become a wolf?' and answered it in no uncertain terms, 'The Italian race is a race of sheep. Eighteen years are not enough to change them. It takes a hundred and eighty, and maybe a hundred and eighty centuries'.

From this perspective, the nationalist and fascist project of nationhood and modernity had come to an end before the disastrous war campaigns sealed the fate of the regime and of Mussolini himself. Indeed, in the night between 24 and 25 July 1943, soon after the Allies had landed in Sicily, Mussolini suffered the humiliation of being put into a minority within his own creation, the National Fascist Party. The next day he was arrested and later taken to the Gran Sasso mountain from where he was liberated by the Germans in a daring raid on 12 September. Mussolini went on to lead the Italian Social Republic (otherwise known as the Republic of Salò) in German-occupied central and northern Italy, which lacked any real degree of autonomy. In the ensuing civil war between fascist and anti-fascist Italians—the latter as part of a national resistance movement—which raged from 1943 to 1945, fighting was harsh and unforgiving, thus at least partially disproving Mussolini's disparaging statement. The civilian population was not spared, becoming the target of reprisals by Germans aided by fascists. Mass killings were carried out on numerous occasions, notably at the Fosse Ardeatine in Rome on 24 March 1944, at Sant'Anna di Stazzema in Tuscany on 12 August 1944 and, at Marzabotto near Bologna between 29 September and 5 October 1944. Yet those who fought to salvage fascist ideals were now in the minority. As for young people, they fought on both sides, holding opposing values and contrasting visions of the nation-state.

The rise and decline of a Christian take on modern nationhood

After the Second World War, the newly formed Christian Democracy Party (DC) elaborated a novel project of modernity epitomized by the endorsement of parliamentary democracy, the defence of civil liberties and human dignity, and the pursuit of international cooperation. The project led to significant developments, including a new constitution, which to this day retains popular support; and Italy's participation in the process of European integration, economic growth, and consumerism.

The Christian democratic stance represented a significant new direction for Italian Catholics, given the support lent by the Catholic Church to the fascist regime. The acceptance of modernity within a liberal-democratic framework later found confirmation in the Second Vatican Council's Pastoral Constitution, *Gaudium et Spes* (1965). Entitled 'Pastoral Constitution on the Church in the Modern World', it contains a clear commitment to the principles of freedom, including freedom of religion ('it is only in freedom that people can turn themselves towards what is good'), human rights ('rights and duties are universal and inviolable'), international cooperation and peace, as well as the rule of law and free elections. The document also stated that economic development and technical progress were to 'be promoted', albeit tempered by a high degree of coordination and regulation to prevent economic insecurity. Thus the 1965 Pastoral Constitution finally overcame the Church's long-standing opposition to modernity and opened up a dialogue with the modern world.

It is not a coincidence that when the process of European integration was set in motion Christian democratic parties were in government in all six countries (Italy, Belgium, the Federal Republic of Germany, France, Luxembourg, and the Netherlands) which signed the Treaty establishing the European Coal and Steel Community in 1951, and later became founder members of the European Economic Community in 1957. The European project allowed these parties to reconcile the Catholic Church's traditional mistrust of national sovereignty with support for personal and political rights and for parliamentary democracy, underpinned by Christian beliefs. In Italy, Alcide De Gasperi, leader of the DC and prime minister from 1945 to 1953, equated European integration with a new myth, the myth of peace that would be offered to young people in place of the 'myth of dictatorship, of force, of the national flag'. Speaking to the senate on 15 November 1950, he stated that the opening of national frontiers went hand in hand with progress, including in the sphere of technology and communications, and with democracy. With considerable foresight, he remarked that he considered the creation of a political, economic, unitary, and federated entity in Europe more realistic than believing the existing frontiers were forever insurmountable.

The DC was also one of the main players responsible for the Italian constitution, developed and approved by a constituent assembly elected on 2 June 1946 by universal suffrage on the basis of proportional representation. Despite the deep differences and divisions separating the Christian democrats from the socialists and the communists, these three parties, which had participated in the resistance movement, shared the view that concentration of power in the executive should be avoided to prevent any authoritarian outcomes and that human, social, and political rights should be unequivocally upheld. The Italian constitution came into effect on 1 January 1948 and has remained in place to this day, if with some not insignificant amendments during that time. Its continuing popularity was confirmed as late as December 2012 when an audience of 12,619,000 watched a TV show entitled 'The Most Beautiful in the World', with reference to the constitutional text, from which actor Roberto Benigni gave a public reading. The show was broadcast in the wake of various demonstrations 'in defence of the Constitution' against what was suspected to be the Berlusconi government's attempt to establish a more authoritarian regime.

The Christian democrats' project of political democratization and economic development was tied in with the retention of traditional social values revolving around the family, religion, and small-scale, tightly knit communities—not least as a bulwark against socialism and communism. To this end, small firms and businesses were prioritized over large-scale corporations. Political regulation of the economy—implemented both directly through the creation of large public holdings and indirectly through a fairly closed system of public–private participations—would ensure social stability and security. Particular attention was paid to the development of the South, with the launch in 1950 of a 'Special Fund for the South' (the 'Cassa per il Mezzogiorno'), aimed at carrying out a programme of 'extraordinary' public works in this area of the country with the ambitious goal of industrializing it and bridging the gap with the North of the country (Figure 3).

Economic growth, partly thanks to membership of the European Economic Community, was successfully achieved, as the country experienced an 'economic miracle' in the late 1950s and 1960s, when GDP grew at a rate of 6 per cent per year, and Italy developed an international reputation for style and innovation. However, growth was accompanied by the inevitable processes of industrialization, urbanization, internal migration (from the South to the North), and, above all, secularization, which went counter to and ultimately superseded the Christian democratic project of modernity. A youth rebellion and a feminist movement challenged traditional Catholic values and pushed for civil liberties, including sexual freedom, contraception, divorce, and abortion. The last two rights were secured after two public referenda in 1974 and 1981 respectively, amid wide social mobilization and in the face of huge opposition from the DC and

3. Inauguration of Italy's first motorway, the Autostrada del Sole, in 1964.

the Catholic Church. A new family law introduced in 1975 established the moral and legal equality of spouses in contrast to the previous regime when the husband had been legally recognized as the head of the family and thus entrusted with ultimate authority.

The Christian democrat belief in cooperation between social classes and between workers and employers also met with a serious setback when a militant workers' movement developed in parallel with the youth and women's movements. Centred on the large factories of the North which had recruited a fresh labour force from the surrounding countryside and from the South, the movement gave rise to a series of strikes, protests, and forms of sabotage, which lasted from the so-called 'Hot Autumn' of 1969 well into the 1970s. It was bent on securing higher wages, better conditions of work, and bargaining rights for workers. There was also a growing revolutionary strand of the movement which sought the abolition of capitalism and its replacement by a socialist society, and which found on this basis a common terrain of action with the youth rebellion.

These radical demands found a partial response in the Italian Communist Party (PCI), whose project of modernity was an alternative both to the Christian democrats and to the 'orthodox' communist regimes dominant in Eastern Europe. By the 1970s the PCI had evolved towards a reformist rather than a revolutionary stance, even though it was only after the fall of the Berlin Wall that it officially renounced its communist ideology. At the time the PCI, led by Enrico Berlinguer, developed a new strand of communism, in collaboration with other West European communist parties, especially the French and Spanish.

Known as 'Eurocommunism', it advocated greater social equality as well as austerity measures coupled with a transition to some form of socialized economy. As Giorgio Napolitano, one of the leaders of the Italian PCI who was to become the Republic's eleventh president (2006–15) put it in 1977, his party believed in 'promoting an effective mass participation in the management of economic, social and political life, transforming economic and social structures, carrying out substantial changes in the power relationship between the classes'. While seemingly gaining ground in the 1970s when economic growth started to slow down, the Italian communists' vision was ultimately displaced by a consumerist and individualist culture, which later led to a turn to the right in the country.

Ironically, if viewed in the light of these various top-down attempts at instilling a shared national identity, Italians were formed by consumer culture thanks to the post-war economic miracle. They increasingly spoke the same language instead of a local dialect due to the impact of television, ate the same food beyond regional variations, dressed in similar ways, and listened to the same music. This was especially the case with the younger generation, as the emerging youth culture led to a specific youth market, epitomized by the ubiquitous Vespa scooter produced for and deliberately marketed to this section of the population. The political violence and terrorism which raged in the country from the late 1960s to the early 1980s at the hands of extreme-right and extreme-left groups inspired by radically anti-capitalist ideologies, attracted considerable support from one section of the youth. However, it could not stop, indeed paradoxically it contributed to, a rising quest for pleasure and entertainment among many other young people and Italians generally.

Modern nationhood as consumerism and marketing

A seductive project of modernization epitomized by media tycoon Silvio Berlusconi has characterized the greater part of the so-called Second Republic (1992 to the present), thanks to a mixture of nationalist themes and an uncritical embracing of consumer and media culture. This has also been the period in which it is possible to detect a widespread sense of apathy, if not disillusionment, with the very notion of modernity, and a growing difficulty in believing in any unifying narratives of progress, sentiments that previously were confined mainly to writers and intellectuals.

The years 1994–2011 marked the rise and triumph of a new style of politics, a flamboyant political personality, and a new narrative of nationhood which celebrated pleasure-seeking, consumption, personal success, prosperity, and freedom. Already anticipated in the trendy and hedonistic lifestyle that established itself in 1980s Milan (famously captured in a 1987 advertisement for an Italian *digestif* which exalted the city as a place 'to live, to dream of, to enjoy'), it was incarnated in Silvio Berlusconi's lifestyle and media. On a personal level, his unswerving optimism, his iconic image as self-made tycoon, and his flaunted sexual prowess appealed to a public seemingly tired of the Catholic and Marxist emphasis on social solidarity and responsibility. Through his media empire, he revolutionized television, offering talk shows, soap operas, games and contests, as well as sports news, all spiced up by the appearance of scantily dressed showgirls (so-called *veline*). For the first time in Italy, television was no longer a medium to educate the public but to entertain it, thus accompanying and contributing to a general decline in civic engagement.

After the collapse of the DC in the early 1990s, in the wake of a huge corruption scandal, Berlusconi formed an entirely new party, Forza Italia ('Come On Italy') in January 1994 and went on to win the general elections in April of that year as part of a centre-right coalition. What had taken Mussolini three years to accomplish (and then only through the use of violence), was achieved in just three months, thanks to the use of media politics to seduce the public.

Berlusconi's political leadership matched his personal lifestyle and media strategy, and indeed was modelled upon them. He personalized politics and 'sold' himself to the public as epitomizing the solution to all of Italy's ills. Just as he had amassed enormous wealth, so would he also be able to make the country rich and prosperous. Following his example, Italians could make it to the top and should aspire to the best. Even his 'vices' were presented as virtues, so that evading tax became a rightful rejection of state interference in personal freedom and entrepreneurship, while self-interest was turned into a justified and legitimate pursuit—people should be entitled to have what they wanted.

The project of modernity associated with Berlusconi's rise to power amounted to what he himself defined as 'a liberal revolution', bearing similarities with the values promoted by Margaret Thatcher in Britain and Ronald Reagan in the USA. In the case of Italy, where liberal ideas and policies after 1945 had been at best merely accommodated within otherwise non-liberal political traditions, placing them at the centre of a new political project was indeed revolutionary. Similar to Thatcherism, neo-liberal ideas were also used to underpin a revival of national pride and allegiance, branded as being in opposition to an 'unpatriotic' left and, increasingly, to a European 'superstate'. However, the liberal vision was never really implemented, mainly because it would have meant attacking and destabilizing vested socio-economic interests or indeed tackling the overblown and underperforming public bureaucracy. In the end, Berlusconi was unable to bridge the gap between his inflated promises of prosperity and the reality of the economic and financial crisis engulfing the country in the early 2010s, which led to his downfall in November 2011.

Berlusconi has often been compared to Mussolini, and his opponents on the left seriously accused him of attempting to set up an authoritarian form of government through a soft 'coup d'état'. Certainly control of the media and propaganda were features of both political projects. Furthermore, Berlusconi and his post-fascist allies promoted a process of historical revisionism in relation to fascist Italy, refuelling long-standing myths on the relatively benign nature of the dictatorship (with the exception of the blot represented by the racial laws). With hindsight, however, the Berlusconi era should perhaps be viewed more as an uncritical celebration of modernity as represented by consumption and spectacle which caught the mood of many Italians than as a strategic project aimed at radically changing the nature of the political system. At any rate, if the latter had indeed been contemplated, it was thwarted by a combination of domestic and EU opposition, and by Berlusconi's own failures.

Italy today: disillusionment with modernity?

Berlusconi's decline left behind a vacuum in terms of powerful and convincing narratives of modernity for binding Italians together. Indeed the notions of 'modernity' and 'modernization' had themselves for some time been challenged in the case of Italy by both domestic and foreign intellectuals. In other words, 'modernity' had been interpreted as a deeply ethnocentric concept, linked to the geopolitical and cultural domination first of Northern European nation-states and afterwards of the United States. The socio-economic and political systems of these countries were identified as indisputable models against which all the other nation-states were by default compared and judged—and generally unfavourably.

Some of the more fundamental criticisms of modernity have come from southern Italian intellectuals who in the 1990s elaborated a current of ideas known as 'Mediterranean thought'. After decades in which the South had been waiting for salvation from the North and from Europe in the form of economic growth and industrialization, intellectuals like Franco Cassano rejected any project of modernity which revolved around technical progress or consumer culture. In their place, alternative values rooted in southern culture and traditions were to be promoted, first and foremost the value of 'slowness', which allows humanity to resist the compression of time and the social acceleration imposed by the current age, dubbed 'turbocapitalism'.

As mentioned in the Introduction, nowadays disillusionment with the idea of modernity goes beyond the works of intellectuals. In stark contrast to neighbouring France, large-scale public works projects have generated widespread opposition, while the Slow Food movement, founded by Carlo Petrini in 1986, has since 1989 developed into a global organization. As he himself stated in an interview given to the British newspaper *The Independent* in 2009, 'The idea of the modern has been superseded; the challenge today is to return to the small scale, the hand-made, to local distribution—because today what we call "modern" is out of date'. In recent years the movement has inspired a campaign to promote 'Zero-Km' products, aimed at offering consumers seasonal goods from the local area.

Disillusionment with modernity has also brought about alternative (negative) readings of the processes of national unification and European integration. The latter in particular has suffered a reversal of popularity. From being the country which invariably produced some of the highest approval ratings of the EU, Italy has turned into the one with the lowest. As in other southern European member states, the EU is in danger of no longer being perceived as a bringer of good politics and material prosperity but as an interfering and dogmatic entity eager to impose austerity measures in order to address the public deficit at the cost of lower standards of living and growing unemployment.

The emergence of diverse currents of thought which reject the idea of a uni-dimensional 'path to modernity' has confirmed Italy's position at the crossroads between a European North and a Mediterranean South. However, it has also exacerbated the difficulty it has always experienced in developing and putting across, both domestically and externally, a convincing narrative of what it means to be Italian and what Italy stands for. In recent years the competing narratives have consisted of the story of austerity, told primarily by the European Union and some domestic parties, and Berlusconi's promise of increased prosperity without the need for sacrifices. Other narratives have provided radical alternatives to modernizing visions. One story has been missing altogether in the public domain: it concerns the nature of contemporary Italy as a multicultural and multi-ethnic society.

With the decline of Berlusconi's project of modernity, can Italians be reconciled to a modernity that for the last decade has not brought material well-being? Or will they heed the message that modernity is a thing of the past? Will cultural and religious diversity be woven into novel understandings of national identity? Perhaps Italy is experiencing a new type of self-reflective modernity, which by questioning the merits of high-speed societies and material growth and by revaluing a Mediterranean perspective may yet promote a dialogue and a fruitful tension between different narratives of who Italians are and where they are heading. This process may also be helped by the fact that a generational transition of power post-Berlusconi was successfully achieved without recourse to violence.

Chapter 3
Governing Italy

A specific strand of controversy and debate surrounding Italy's path to modernity has focused on its political system and style of government. In Liberal Italy, we can detect two styles of governing. On the one hand, ruling with an iron fist at home and promoting an aggressive foreign and colonial policy, as attempted by Prime Minister Francesco Crispi in the 1880s and early 1890s. On the other hand, governing by consensus through compromise with social forces and reliance on a certain parliamentary practice that became known as *trasformismo* ('transformism'). This consisted of securing a majority in Parliament thanks to the support of individual deputies or groups of deputies above and beyond their party affiliation. Corrupt and nepotistic practices helped 'oil' the machinery of power and secure the stability of incumbent governments. The term *trasformismo* has since proved extremely resilient with political commentators and in the media, and has been used repeatedly at different political junctures as a metaphor for the allegedly distorted and outdated Italian model of parliamentary democracy.

These styles of governing were replicated (and exacerbated) after the fall of the Liberal State. Mussolini resorted to a full-blown dictatorship in order to impose total control at home while systematically pursuing war abroad from the 1930s onwards. He attacked Ethiopia in 1935 to secure for Italy a large colonial empire, sided with Franco during the Spanish civil war, and joined forces with Nazi Germany in July 1940, despite Italy's military unpreparedness. Yet the reality of fascist rule was quite different from its totalitarian goals, and client politics did not come to an end during the regime.

The fascist dictatorship and its tragic epilogue convinced post-war political elites of the need to put in place a series of checks and balances in order to disperse power and prevent its being concentrated in one single leader. Matters were further complicated by the fact that in the post-war period Italy was a 'microcosm' of the Cold War due to the presence of the two main antagonists—the Communists and anti-Communists. In the immediate aftermath of war (1945–7) the country was run by a government of national unity, which included the Socialist and Communist Parties in alliance with the Christian Democratic Party (DC), by virtue of their participation in the resistance and their anti-fascist credentials. After this initial period, however, the Communist Party was relegated to the role of permanent opposition, while the DC were always in government. Hence Italy's political system came under scrutiny for constituting a 'blocked democracy'.

The 'anomaly' of this system lasted until 1992, when, following the end of the Cold War and a huge corruption scandal, the traditional parties collapsed and proportional representation was replaced by a predominantly majoritarian or 'first past the post' electoral system. This promoted the formation of two coalition 'poles', the centre-left and the centre-right, alternating in power. However, any hope that this would be deemed a clear sign of Italy finally achieving political modernization proved short-lived, since the two main coalitions appeared internally unstable, often unable to carry out effective and decisive policies and prone to behave as sworn enemies. Silvio Berlusconi himself, as we saw earlier, appeared to be an odd mixture of old and new. His use of the media and his charismatic and highly personal style of leadership were undoubtedly innovative, while his corrupt methods and his numerous criminal charges were much less so. Furthermore, the mutual antagonism between left and right was at times judged as a screen behind which the political class (recently dubbed the *casta* or 'caste', with reference to its being both united and untouchable) was seen to behave in a uniformly corrupt manner, bent on safeguarding its own interests and survival rather than working for the good of the country. In short, transformism lurked once again behind the apparent overhaul of Italian politics.

The origins and resilience of *trasformismo*

Transformism was first experienced in the 1870s and later developed into a sophisticated art by Prime Minister Giovanni Giolitti in the early 1900s. In 1876, the year the moderate left was able to form its first government, new Prime Minister Agostino Depretis publicly stated his wish that he would be able to promote 'that transformation of the parties, that unification of all the Liberal forces within the Chamber, which will contribute to form the hoped-for stable majority'. In fact he went on to form a solid government without the need for support from other parties. However, in 1882, following a widening of voting rights, Depretis ended up forming a majority with the support of a group of former representatives of the right, led by Marco Minghetti. In a speech to the Chamber of Deputies delivered in May 1883, Minghetti defended his decision to prop up a leftist government, based on three main arguments. The first was that an effective government needed a broad majority in Parliament. The second was that, notwithstanding the principle that in a constitutional political system there should be two parties alternating in government, this only applied if the two parties in question represented two alternative visions, and in Italy this was not the case. In his view, a conservative party as such did not exist, and both right and left represented variants of the Liberal Party. Third, he stated that Italy, like other European countries, had witnessed the rise of extreme radical parties which posed a threat to the Liberal system.

In these circumstances, Minghetti proudly reaffirmed his decision and rejected the derogatory expression 'transformism' which had replaced Depretis's positive term 'transformation', claiming that it was possible to form coalition governments while remaining faithful to one's own political principles.

Minghetti's arguments accurately reflected the political situation in Italy following the aftermath of the Unification. With the social question increasingly looming large and Catholics being forbidden to participate in elections, the differences between the heirs of the Risorgimento's moderates and democrats had effectively shrunk, thereby facilitating their coming together in government, as opposed to forming two alternative parties vying for power. Consequently, from then on parliamentary majorities were formed with the support of various groups of right, centre, and left Liberal deputies, while other groups stood in opposition.

By the time Giovanni Giolitti came to dominate Italian politics—he was prime minister in 1892–3 and again from 1903 to 1914, save a few brief interruptions—it was no longer simply a question of whether the heirs of the Risorgimento 'parties' should work together or not. The main questions revolved around the attitude the Liberal Party should adopt towards the radical parties on the left and how the latter would respond, and on whether an alternative parliamentary pole would be able (or indeed allowed) to form. With the Catholics still out of the political game, the main contender was the Socialist Party founded in 1892 by lawyer Filippo Turati, his partner Anna Kulishoff, and philosophy professor Antonio Labriola. The Socialist Party was an urban-rural movement with pockets of strength in the industrial cities of the North and the capitalist farming region of Emilia-Romagna. It benefitted from the rise of trade union organizations as well as workers' and farmers' resistance leagues capable of promoting strikes and other collective forms of agitation aimed at raising working class living standards and securing their rights.

The initial reaction of the Liberal governments was to resort to social and political repression. Strikes and other protests were often dealt with by the police and the army through the use of brutal methods, particularly during the premiership of Francesco Crispi and above all in the period from 1896 to 1900, known as the 'End of Century Crisis'. This was both a social and a political crisis. At a social level, various popular riots around the country against a rise in the price of bread culminated in a revolt in Milan in 1898, repressed by troops led by General Fiorenzo Bava Beccaris by firing on the crowds, causing at least eighty casualties, according to official figures. At a political level, the right-wing Liberal governments that followed each other in rapid succession resorted to devising ways to restrict the suffrage or limit civil liberties. Indeed political repression followed the Milan riots with the arrest of socialist leaders, the closure of trade union organizations, and the curbing of the press. The king, Humbert I, who had decorated Bava Beccaris for 'great service...paid to the institutions and civilization', was himself assassinated by an anarchist in 1900. In the same year, political elections saw the extreme left jump from sixty-seven to ninety-six seats out of a total of 508, thanks mainly to a significant rise in support for the Socialist Party, which increased the number of its seats from sixteen to thirty-three.

According to Sidney Sonnino, a long-standing Liberal politician and outspoken critic of *trasformismo*, the crisis had come about as a consequence of the primacy Parliament had acquired over the executive and the executive over the monarchy. In an article entitled 'Torniamo allo Statuto' ('Let's go back to the Statute'), Sonnino advocated as a solution the rigid application of the original 1848 Piedmontese Liberal Statute—which had become the Italian constitution after the Unification—thereby giving the king full executive powers, including the right to ratify laws and to appoint and dismiss ministers. This would have freed prime ministers from the need to establish a majority in Parliament by cobbling together groups of deputies in the absence of clearly defined political alternatives. Yet going back to a 19th-century-style constitutional monarchy in the face of the birth of 20th-century-style mass organizations did not seem to many to be a feasible or desirable solution.

So it was that a modified and modernized version of *trasformismo* devised by Giolitti ended up proving to be fairly effective in securing stable governing majorities in the context of rising radical ideologies, and social and territorial divisions. Giolitti's strategy consisted of inducing the moderate wing of the Socialist Party, led by Turati himself, to support his governments in Parliament, in exchange for social reforms, a programme of nationalization of the railways, telephone, and life insurance industries, public works, and a tolerant attitude towards labour strikes, all of which would lead to a gradual improvement in working conditions and living standards of the lower classes.

The success of the strategy depended on a series of external circumstances as well as political leadership. The fact that Italy experienced sustained economic development during the period 1896–1914 (albeit with a slowdown after 1907), obviously contributed significantly to Giolitti's capacity to deliver reforms and to the willingness of employers to grant wage increases. On the socialist front, the predominance of the moderate wing over the radical and revolutionary currents within the Italian Socialist Party, which lasted with mixed fortunes until 1912, helped to prop up Giolitti's governments. Finally, the absence of other significant political players also played a part. However, as discussed in Chapter 1, from 1910 onwards new political groups and movements had already started to challenge Giolitti and his politics, despite his ability to juggle these forces to obtain support in the short term (Figure 4).

While the overall judgement of historians on the Giolittian system tends to be overwhelmingly positive, various criticisms have repeatedly been raised. One of the main criticisms, which at the

4. Satirical cartoon of Giovanni Giolitti from *L'Asino* magazine,
14 May 1911. It depicts the Italian statesman showing one face to the
middle classes and another one to the workers.

time was forcefully expressed by southern Italian intellectuals like the socialists Arturo Labriola and Gaetano Salvemini, concerned the dual nature of his approach to politics—progressive and tolerant in the North but conservative and repressive in the South. It was no coincidence that in the South the Liberal governments were able to rely on strong majorities at successive elections, as trade unions and labour organizations were much weaker and employers much less prone to making concessions. Another criticism targeted Giolitti's reliance on corruption and nepotism to gain votes, a practice used systematically in the South. The outcome was that the southern regions did not benefit significantly from Giolitti's reforms and in fact experienced unprecedented levels of emigration in the years he ruled the country.

Finally, a fundamental criticism is based on Giolitti's inability to promote a radical reform of the social system, by breaking up the excessive power exercised by landowners in the South and in the Po Valley, or indeed of the political system, so as to allow for an alternation of parties in government. In particular, he appeared not to understand the transformation of the country into a democracy in which the masses had the right to vote, and consequently he failed to turn the Liberal Party into a modern organization with a wide appeal. Admittedly, it was only after the electoral reform he himself introduced in 1912 that the electorate jumped from roughly two million to over eight million. However, the trend towards a widening of the suffrage had already been in place.

Beyond these debates, the main issue concerns the longevity of *trasformismo* but also its shortcomings. The system clearly proved pliable and adaptable, allowing for effective, even reformist, governing from the centre, despite the fluid manner in which majorities were formed. However, the governments set up through this system tended to depend quite heavily on a favourable economic trend as they had to be able to satisfy disparate groups of supporters who did not necessarily subscribe to the same political values or goals. At times of economic recession, *trasformismo* tended to unravel, leaving in its wake radical left and right groups which sought to replace it not through alternative parliamentary majorities but through more or less drastic authoritarian solutions or revolutionary movements.

The breakdown of governance following the First World War

After the First World War the governing system experienced a serious crisis which not even Giolitti, called back as prime minister in 1920 to perform the old magic of reconciling political enemies, was able to overcome. His Liberal Party emerged from the war severely weakened in electoral terms following the introduction of universal male suffrage. It formed a series of governments which proved unable to overcome Italy's socio-political divisions, not least because the party's continuing belief in parliamentary politics, compromise, and negotiations clashed with the uncompromising attitudes of most other political groups.

In 1919 the Socialist Party was the nearest thing Italy had to a modern mass party. It was dominated by a revolutionary wing, which looked forward to a Soviet-style revolution. The so-called *biennio rosso* ('two red years') of 1919–20 represented a period of social unrest, with mass strikes, demonstrations, and food riots in Italy's main cities. Yet the Socialist Party did very little to promote a coherent strategy aimed at seizing power in the country and succeeded instead in creating widespread feelings of fear and revenge among the middle classes and employers. The Catholic Party, founded in 1919 by a Sicilian priest, Don Luigi Sturzo, also enjoyed a wide following, but its electoral base was restricted to a few northern areas and it was divided into various currents, which had a paralysing effect. In addition, the party did not have the full backing of the Vatican, which considered it both too radical and too lay, thereby depriving it of an important source of legitimacy.

As for the nationalists, they were able to exploit the myth of 'mutilated victory', in other words, the feeling that Italy was being unfairly treated at the Paris Peace Conference of 1919, in order to discredit the Liberal governments for their supposedly weak stance at Versailles. Under the leadership of the poet Gabriele D'Annunzio, a group of nationalists resorted to direct action by organizing the seizure of Fiume (Rijeka) in September 1919. In March of the same year, Mussolini had thrown the gauntlet into the political arena when he founded the fascist movement with a leftist programme revolving around workers' rights, progressive taxation, and anti-big-business measures. When the movement failed to gain a single seat in Parliament at the 1919 election, Mussolini shifted to the right, promising lower taxes for businesses, discipline in the workplace, and foreign expansionism.

In 1920 the fascist movement had a breakthrough in the Po Valley, previously dominated by the socialists, thanks to a systematic use of violence against leftist supporters and an alliance with landowners. In this area, new local fascist leaders (so-called *Ras*) emerged, who were extremely radical and bent on establishing a fascist dictatorship. Prime Minister Giolitti mistakenly believed that he could turn a blind eye to fascist violence as a means of taming the more radical socialists. He also attempted to resume his pre-war strategy of bringing political opponents into the fold of the parliamentary system and to this end struck electoral deals with both nationalists and fascists. The strategy backfired badly. Mussolini's party gained political legitimacy as well as thirty-five seats at the 1921 elections but this did not put an end to fascist violence.

In short, the incoherent strategy pursued by the Socialist Party and the perceived weakness of successive Liberal governments created a political space for a new radical movement. In the face of growing fascist aggressiveness, persisting internal divisions, and weak governments, but also thanks to Mussolini's opportunism and a deep misunderstanding of the nature of this new movement among its opponents, fascism became the successful solution to Italy's post-war crisis. Liberal governments after Giolitti continued to fail to act against its violence, while Mussolini promised a return to law and order. The new pope, Pius XI, who was elected in February 1922, appeared to signal his approval of a government which would include the fascists. Industrialists and landowners viewed fascism's anti-socialist tactics with favour. In this context, the famous 'March on Rome' of 28 October 1922, whereby the fascist 'squads' were to take over control of the city, was a rather peaceful affair rather than a full-blown coup d'état, and the king himself asked Mussolini to lead a coalition government.

Fascism then proceeded to consolidate its power through prevarication and violence. On 10 June 1924, social-democratic MP Giacomo Matteotti, who had denounced fascist violence during the electoral campaign, was kidnapped and later assassinated. His murder, clearly perpetrated by fascists, almost certainly with Mussolini's knowledge, was met by widespread moral revulsion in the country while a protest was staged by anti-fascist deputies. Faced with the risk of being ousted from power, Mussolini gave way to the radical elements within his party and embarked on the path towards a dictatorship.

Fascism now had full powers to mould the nation in accordance to its cultural and political ideology, a project that ultimately failed, as discussed in Chapter 1. In terms of its style of governing, however, there were elements of continuity with Liberal Italy. Indeed, local politics, patronage, and corruption continued to play an important role in the governing of the country during the regime. The fascist party, in particular, failed to promote a new politics or inspire by example which partly explains the concentration of powers in Mussolini himself and his near-deification as father of the nation through the cult of the Duce. Conversely, the regime left a deep legacy on various aspects of politics and policy-making in post-1945 Italy as well as in terms of its popular memory.

A 'blocked democracy'

Between 1945 and 1992 Italy was dominated by the DC but, thanks to a highly proportional electoral system, representation over the entire political spectrum was ensured, from the neo-fascist Movimento Sociale Italiano (MSI) on the right to the Communist Party on the left. Formed in 1942, the DC replaced the Partito Popolare Italiano, founded in 1919 by Luigi Sturzo but banned by Mussolini in 1926. Compared to its predecessor, it benefitted from the Vatican's newly found commitment to democracy and solid support for the formation of Catholic parties.

As the 1946 referendum settled the issue of Italy's form of government by abolishing the Savoy monarchy, tainted by its earlier support for Mussolini, so the general elections of 1948 proved crucial in determining the future political set-up of the country. In a tense confrontation with the left 'Popular Democratic Front' (made up of the Socialist and Communist Parties), the DC triumphed at these elections. It was supported by the Church and the USA, and able to rely on the associations and networks around 'Catholic Action' which had survived the fascist clampdown on all opposition groups. Despite obtaining 48.8 per cent of the votes and 305 seats out of 547, the DC began a trend of governing in alliance with smaller parties on the right and centre in order to avoid being accused of attempting to recreate a one-party regime.

While ostensibly a democratic system with free elections and a free press, Italy did not witness any alternation of the parties in power. The high frequency of reshuffles and permutations within the governing coalitions meant that cabinets often lasted for less than one year, yet political stability was ensured by the continuing presence of the DC (known as the 'White Whale') at the helm of political power. Also, the DC's allies were generally rewarded with minor government offices, whose total figure was often deliberately inflated. This allowed the party to retain both the most important posts and roughly the same number of ministers.

The country's perceived fragile position at the onset of the Cold War, especially due to the presence of the largest communist party in Western Europe, largely accounts for its 'blocked democracy' and also goes some way towards explaining why Italy was not 'de-fascistized' after the war, unlike Germany. While Italian officials strove to exculpate the population and underplay fascist atrocities, the Allies themselves avoided extraditing fascist war criminals to Yugoslavia or publicly prosecuting them in show trials. In order to promote pacification, the 1945–7 government of national unity tolerated the formation of a neo-fascist party in 1946 and in the same year the leader of the Communist Party himself, Palmiro Togliatti, signed as minister of justice an amnesty for many political crimes committed by fascists. As a result, the worst aspects of the fascist regime were not openly disclosed and debated. In place of collective responsibility, a myth of the regime as having been fairly benign and of Italians as innocent victims of Mussolini became prevalent.

After a decade of open political confrontation with the parties of the left and trade unions, the 1960s ushered in a period of government by consensus, leading to the so-called 'Opening to the Left', that is to say the incorporation of the Socialist Party, led by Pietro Nenni, into the governing coalitions. Officially sanctioned by both the American President John F. Kennedy and Pope John XXIII, the Opening to the Left was the brainchild of Aldo Moro, the DC leader and statesman, who realized that new demands of society and the continuing appeal of left-wing parties necessitated a change of direction. Furthermore, detaching the Socialist Party from the Communist Party had the advantage of leaving the latter isolated and weaker. Italy was one of a very few places in Europe where the socialists and communists collaborated after the Second World War, but the alliance collapsed with the Soviet invasion of Hungary in 1956, which provoked revulsion among many leftist supporters.

Under pressure from social and trade union movements, the new centre-left coalition governments introduced a series of social reforms—from health care to pensions, tax reform to the school system, and the 1970 Workers' Statute—and developed a more tolerant attitude towards strikes and other forms of industrial unrest, which in turn led to rising standards of living.

There are some similarities between Moro's strategy of 'Opening to the Left' and Giolitti's strategy of coming to an understanding with the moderate wing of the Socialist Party in the 1900s. In both cases, the aim was threefold: to strengthen parliamentary support for the government; to widen the social consensus through reforms that would appeal to a broader section of the electorate; and to isolate the extreme wings. In both cases an expanding economy allowed for greater spending on the part of the governments while they came under severe criticism for establishing patron–client ties with the electorate and promoting corrupt deals which included turning a blind eye to, or even becoming enmeshed in, organized crime activities.

In the 1970s, however, political stability gave way to instability. On the one hand, the growing popularity of the Communist Party and increased mobilization on the part of student, worker, and women's movements put new demands upon government and new strains on a political system and a society which until then had acquiesced to traditional Catholic values. The DC and its allies responded by introducing new reforms, such as the 1970 reform establishing a regional tier of government (already envisaged by the 1948 constitution), but they were also seriously divided over civil rights issues, especially the 1970 law legalizing divorce, promoted by the Socialist Party but opposed by the Catholic Church and many in the DC. This led to a highly divisive referendum in 1974 which showed the extent to which the country had become secularized, to the surprise of both Catholics and non-Catholics, as 59.1 per cent of voters chose to retain the divorce law. This percentage went way beyond the proportion of the electorate who supported the left and lay parties, testifying to the exercising of a free choice on the part of voters no longer rigidly aligned to long-standing party loyalties.

Political instability was exacerbated by the ugly outbreak of ideologically inspired terrorist movements on both the left and the right. Despite being home-grown, Italian terrorism was caught up in the logic of the Cold War and was, at least in part, manipulated by wider international forces. It consisted of both a sustained bombing campaign carried out in crowded places and an 'armed struggle' against the State perpetrated by left and right groups. In December 1969, bomb attacks took place in Rome and Milan, one of which, in Milan's Piazza Fontana, resulted in seventeen people dead and several badly injured. The Milan bombing heralded the beginning of a murky terrorist campaign and inspired the famous 1970 satirical play *Morte accidentale di un anarchico* ('Accidental Death of an Anarchist') by Dario Fo, viewed by over half a million Italians during the first two years of production.

To this day it remains unclear who masterminded this attack or what the aims were. Responsibility for the attacks, in fact, largely went unclaimed by any groups. However, several judicial trials lasting well into the 2000s, established that these bombings were part of a wider strategy—generally known as the 'Strategy of Tension'—which aimed at creating an atmosphere of terror in the country in order to impose a more authoritarian regime of proven anti-Communist mettle. The strategy, which relied on the active as well as passive connivance of a wide network of more or less secretive domestic and international anti-Communist forces, depended on neo-fascist terrorist groups carrying out bloody attacks designed to put the blame upon left organizations, thereby justifying a clampdown on civil and political liberties. If successful, it would once again have steered the country away from consensual politics and towards ruling with an iron fist.

By contrast, the threatening divisions and organized violence of the 1970s convinced Aldo Moro of the need to replicate his previous strategy under the new circumstances and hence come to an understanding with the Italian Communist Party, so as to reinforce the government and isolate the radical wings operating on the extreme left and right. This rapprochement led to the so-called Historic Compromise (1976–9), an agreement between the two parties on the basis of which the Communists were prepared to give external support in Parliament to a new DC-led government.

On 16 March 1978, while on his way to Parliament where a new government headed by Giulio Andreotti with the external support of the Communists was to be sworn in, Aldo Moro was kidnapped by the Red Brigades, the most notorious left terrorist group who considered the Historic Compromise an aberration and further proof that the Communist Party had betrayed its original revolutionary ideals. The Italian government refused to have any dealings with the terrorists but also failed to find Moro despite staging an unprecedented surveillance and security operation. On 9 May 1978 the Red Brigades dumped Moro's body in a car in Rome, symbolically half way between the headquarters of the DC and the Communist Party. Moro's assassination marked the beginning of the end for left-wing terrorism but it also left a long-standing legacy of controversies and divisions in Italian culture and society.

There are many both in Italy and abroad who do not accept the official version of events, partly in light of the puzzling circumstances surrounding his kidnapping and period of captivity. They also point to the fact that Moro's strategy was strongly opposed within his own party as well as by the USA and other NATO countries because it would destabilize the international political order. Refusing to believe that the Red Brigades acted alone, sceptics maintain that, as in the case of the 'Strategy of Tension', the murder of Aldo Moro can only be explained with reference to the country's controversial role in the Cold War. The role of the secret Masonic Lodge P2, discovered in May 1981, has also repeatedly been called into question, since it included important political, military, and intelligence figures and was found to be involved in corrupt deals as well as in funding terrorist groups.

Moro's death soon put an end to the Historic Compromise. In the 1980s, the popularity of the Communist Party started to wane, while the governments were once again entrusted to centre-left coalitions which included the Socialists but excluded the Communists. By then, however, the drive for reform had started to slow down, and the decade also saw a spiralling of the public deficit, as governing through consensus meant relying upon increased public borrowing. There was also a parallel expansion of nepotistic and corrupt practices.

The extent to which such practices involved shady dealings between politicians and organized crime, especially the Sicilian Mafia, emerged clearly at the time of the so-called 'maxi-trial' of 1986–7. Thanks to Mafiosi turned supergrasses and to the brave work of magistrates Giovanni Falcone and Paolo Borsellino, 474 members and leaders of Cosa Nostra were charged and 360 convicted. The Mafia reacted by waging war on the magistrates responsible for the trial and in 1992 both Falcone and Borsellino were killed in acts of revenge. Hence the restored political stability rested upon fragile foundations and was to be swept away by the political earthquake whose tremors began with the fall of the Berlin Wall in 1989 and ended with the 1992 corruption scandal known as 'Kickback City'. Italy's 'First Republic' had come to an end.

Italy's 'Second Republic'

The collapse of the First Republic established after 1945 led to a complete overhaul of the Italian political system and the disappearance of its main protagonists, from the DC to the

Communist Party, and from the Socialist Party to the neo-fascist MSI. Once the bulk of the Communist Party had renounced Marxist ideology and the bulk of the MSI had turned its back on fascism, the path was open for a thaw in Italy's blocked democracy through the legitimization of all main parties as potential partners in governing coalitions.

Furthermore, the process of secularization of Italian society had weakened the Catholic–lay divide, so much so that the DC split into separate wings, one of which joined an alliance with the former Communists, hence allowing for coalitions to be established along the conventional centre-right and centre-left axis. This process was facilitated by a new electoral system introduced in 1993, designed to promote the alternation of parties in government.

The outcome was a partially successful transition to a bi-polar political system, with two coalitions alternating in government, something not experienced in the First Republic. Since the 1994 elections, alternating coalitions have arguably constituted the most important development in Italian politics. In 1994, Berlusconi established an electoral alliance comprising his own party, Forza Italia, the separatist Lega Nord (Northern League), and the post-fascist Alleanza Nazionale (AN), as well as minor parties formed after the collapse of the DC. This was no mean feat, considering Berlusconi professed neo-liberal ideas, AN was traditionally in favour of a strong centralized State, and the Lega Nord was regionalist and federalist. In 1996 the left was able to respond by establishing the so-called Ulivo coalition (Olive Tree), headed by Romano Prodi, a former university professor and manager of public enterprises. The coalition comprised the mainstream centre-left party—Democratic Party of the Left, later just Democratic Party—and a number of smaller parties to its right and its left.

The two coalitions proved popular with the electorate. A centre-right government was elected in 1994, a centre-left one in 1996, a centre-right one in 2001, another centre-left one in 2006, and a centre-right one in 2008. While only one government, headed by Berlusconi, ran its full course of five years, the coalitions managed to provide a degree of stability and were able to introduce some economic and social reforms. However, on the negative side, the electoral reform approved in 1993 did not succeed in reducing the number of parties or in ensuring the dominance of the mainstream ones. Rather, it appeared to strengthen the extreme parties, which enjoyed a high degree of leverage within each coalition both in terms of influencing policies and in terms of holding governments to ransom. Thus it was the Lega Nord which caused the fall of the first Berlusconi government in 1994, after just a few months in power, and it was Rifondazione Comunista ('Communist Refoundation') which brought down the first Prodi government in 1998, even though the centre-left coalition remained in power under a new prime minister.

Berlusconi's governments focused primarily on lowering the fiscal pressure, reforming the State along federalist lines, and curbing immigration. These reforms were approved in ways that demonstrated considerable discipline within the coalition yet they yielded only modest results. Despite Berlusconi often blaming the Italian political system and the constitution for allowing too many players to veto decision-making, both in Parliament and outside it, the limited effectiveness of his governments in terms of policy-making was in large part due to the 'populist' character of his own party and of the Northern League. Populism refers to parties which constantly appeal to 'the people' against the established elites, rely on charismatic leaders, and tend to espouse radical policies or make extravagant promises to the electorate which they have difficulty fulfilling once in power. A typical example was Berlusconi's promise in 1994 to create a million jobs within a year. While a political phenomenon widely experienced throughout Europe in the last few decades, populism seemed to find a fertile terrain in Italy at an early stage.

As for the centre-left coalitions, the 1996–2001 government oversaw a heroic effort to bring down Italy's chronic public debt and qualify for entry into the EU's single currency in 1998. It also carried out a modest programme of privatization and simplification of the country's cumbersome bureaucracy. However, the centre-left government's 'federalist' law in 2001, approved by the citizens in a referendum, proved controversial at the time and has since been criticized for contributing to inflation of the costs of regional governments. While less prone to populist traits, these governments were hampered by having to deal with a high number of partners. Thus the second Prodi government lasted only two years and in this period it had to face considerable tension and friction among the nine parties that made up the coalition. The quarrelsome nature of the centre-left governments progressively reduced their ability to implement effective long-term reforms.

In view of the limited effectiveness of the coalition governments in terms of decision-making, there are many who believe that the bi-polar system has not worked properly and that Italy may yet have to abandon it, returning to a system where the centre parties form a coalition, leaving the extreme parties out—just like in the First Republic. What are the signs that this may be the case?

First, we need to look at the relationship between Parliament and government. Italy has traditionally been a parliamentary democracy where the executive has weak decision-making powers, and where party loyalty and discipline are difficult to enforce. Since the 1990s, different governments have attempted to increase their control over Parliament with some degree of success. Indeed, according to political scientist Sergio Fabbrini (2012), Italy has experienced a transition 'from a parliament-centred to a government-centred system'.

The government headed by Matteo Renzi and established in 2014, for instance, was able to pass a series of reforms, including a new electoral law and a controversial reform of the labour market, at relatively high speed, despite opposition within Parliament and within his own party, as well as from the trade unions. However, Renzi's hand was weakened after a pact with Berlusconi on constitutional reforms came to an end in January 2015, given his slender majority in the senate. Furthermore, his government was at risk of defections. The autonomy and independence of Italian MPs are sanctioned by the constitution and they have the right to vote according to their free will. More importantly, they have the right to change allegiance once elected to Parliament. The latter trend—typical of transformism—was significantly on the increase after 2008, with 261 transfers taking place between 2008 and 2013, and 235 changes involving 185 MPs between March 2013 and March 2015.

Second, it is often considered that transformism goes hand in hand with a high level of corruption and patron–client relationships, which ensure political stability and parliamentary loyalty and also generate considerable resources at the disposal of existing parties. In 1992, as we saw, the Italian First Republic came to an end under the weight of a huge corruption scandal involving the governing parties, especially the DC and the Socialist Party, but also, albeit to a much lesser extent, the Communist Party, the main party in opposition. The scandal revealed the existence of underground networks linking political parties to the financial and business world and even to organized crime. The new bi-polar political system was expected to put an end to such practices yet various scandals repeatedly broke out at local levels, showing that secret networks carrying out corrupt dealings involved both majority and opposition parties. Hence the nickname of *La Casta* ('Caste') coined with reference to the entire political class in a book written by journalists Sergio Rizzo and Gian Antonio Stella and published in 2007 which became a bestseller. In these circumstances, the virtuous nature of a bi-polar configuration was put into question, and support for a return to the Italian tradition of governing from the centre increased among intellectuals and political experts.

Third, by 2015 the bi-polar configuration of the political system was no longer clear-cut. On the one hand, a process of fragmentation appeared to have put paid to the centre-right coalition. Berlusconi's Forza Italia was in disarray while after 2013 the Northern League made substantial electoral gains at its expense but it also adopted an even more radical stance against both immigration and the EU. On the other hand, a new player had come to the fore, the Movimento 5 Stelle (5 Star Movement), headed by ex-comedian Beppe Grillo, which surprised everyone by getting 25 per cent of the votes at the 2013 general elections. This was an anti-establishment, anti-Euro, anti-politics, anti-corruption party in ways that recalled the early Lega Nord, as it appealed to 'the people' against the elites and claimed to have overcome traditional left–right divisions. In place of two main coalitions, therefore, there were three main players—Lega Nord, Movimento 5 Stelle, and the Democratic Party headed by Matteo Renzi.

Fourth, the new electoral law which in 2015 replaced the previous one introduced in 2005 envisaged awarding a majority in Parliament to the party with the highest number of votes. Promoted by Renzi but initially favoured also by Berlusconi, the law seemed designed to ensure the alternation in power of stable governments based on clearly dominant mainstream parties, no longer being held to ransom by minor coalition parties. However, by the time the law was approved the effects of the new system had become unpredictable, given the unstable political set-up and the crisis engulfing Forza Italia. Thus many commentators argued that the Democratic Party would win the next election in a straight fight with radical alternative parties and end up governing from the centre.

If this were the case, Italy's political system would have gone full circle. As the well-known political scientist Angelo Panebianco remarked in the *Corriere della Sera* newspaper in November 2011, following the collapse of the Berlusconi government in the wake of the global financial crisis: 'The Berlusconi era may turn out to have been an interlude between the end of the DC and its rebirth'. However, neither Forza Italia nor even the Democratic Party seems able to inherit the dominant role played by the DC, due in large part to the Cold War and to the moral imperative not to let the Communists into the driving seat. A more likely outcome would therefore be a return to a renewed form of *trasformismo*.

Only the future will tell whether Italy will be able to refine the bi-polar model established after the fall of the First Republic and increase the decision-making powers of the executive or fall back upon tested practices of bargaining among political elites and in Parliament, in the absence of straightforward and clear-cut dynamics between majority and opposition. At the present time, there appears to be less marked confidence in the possibility of achieving a 'modern' democracy through the establishment of a bi-polar system. Conversely, the consensual model of the First Republic has been re-evaluated in a more positive light. In this context, the advantages and disadvantages of each political model can be debated and assessed in a less charged and polemical manner.

Chapter 4
'Made in Italy'

Despite lacking raw materials and still being heavily dependent on agriculture in the early 20th century, Italy managed to become the fifth most industrialized economy in the world by the 1980s. Economic modernization, at least with reference to post-war Italy, would seem both undeniable and uncontroversial. The economic miracle of the 1960s, in particular, was accompanied by social phenomena typically associated with the process of modernization, including urbanization, the predominance of the nuclear family, mass consumerism, and mass transport based on private car ownership. This was the time when Italian design became known the world over, combining creativity with craftsmanship and ranging from everyday goods like kitchen utensils and appliances to luxury products like designer-label fashion and sports cars. While politics stagnated and even descended into violence, the country was turning into a global leader in innovation.

In the 1980s, Italy's strong international ranking and dynamic, export-oriented industries led to lavish praise being poured upon its novel manufacturing model. This centred on the predominance of small-scale family firms in a number of industrial districts which were judged to be more flexible, innovative, and specialized than the increasingly obsolete Fordist model of mass production. Indeed, the Italian system of production was hailed as the model to be imitated in authoritative English-language textbooks on business and management studies.

Despite these achievements, the economic sphere has also been caught up in the debate over the country's allegedly elusive modernization and this in turn has reverberated in the socio-political sphere. Various features of the Italian economy have been judged in need of an overhaul, ranging from the 'excessive' weight of small-scale family firms, the over-reliance on traditional manufacturing, the low level of productivity and competitiveness, to the dependence of the South on the public sector. This debate found a new momentum in the 1990s, when the economic system was challenged by the process of globalization and the need to cut costs in the face of increasing competition from Asian countries.

These difficulties, coupled with the emergence of the regionalist (and increasingly xenophobic) Northern League party, whose strongholds coincided with the areas of small-scale industry, led to a serious rethinking of the 'virtues' of this type of industrialization. Now it was blamed not only for losing steam and clinging to outdated systems of production but also for being inextricably associated with parochial and inward-looking small-town communities, resistant to social change and liberal values. The Northern League was also responsible for resuscitating long-standing prejudices towards southern Italy and its inhabitants, damning the region as a parasite living off northern wealth. Italy's subsequent cycle of sluggish growth and recession further contributed to the revival of notions of decline, applied to the country as a whole rather than being limited to the South.

There is no doubt that the Italian economy was in the doldrums for much of the 1990s and 2000s. In the two decades 1990–2010, GDP rose by less than 1 per cent per year on average and in the first half of the 2010s it actually slid backwards. In 2015, GDP started to rise again, after several months of negative growth, but even then the country lagged behind the rest of the Eurozone.

While this chapter cannot answer the question of whether Italy can reverse the economic decline of the last two and a half decades, it will assess the Italian economy's strong and weak features since the first spurt of industrialization in the late 19th century and discuss the various attempts made to tackle its recent weaknesses.

Early industrialization

Italy's early industrial development was largely restricted to the north-western regions, the so-called 'Industrial Triangle' encompassing Milan, Turin, and Genoa, where a few large private companies stood out at the beginning of the 20th century: Fiat, Montecatini, Olivetti, Pirelli. Italy's industrial take-off was slow to begin. In the period following the Unification, governments adopted a policy of free trade and laissez-faire, which had the unfortunate outcome of leaving the South exposed to both domestic and foreign competition, whereas previously its industries had benefitted from State protection. A sustained expansion of the railway system contributed significantly to the creation of an internal market but did not in itself promote economic growth. At that time, Italy's most important industrial sector was textiles: silk, cotton, and wool manufacturing. In the 1860s, silk accounted for about a quarter of total exports.

In the late 1870s, and even more so in the late 1880s, the governments resorted to introducing tariffs on foreign goods so as to protect Italian industries and encourage the growth of 'heavy' manufacturing, such as metalworking, shipbuilding, and engineering, considered to be strategic for political as well as economic reasons. The period that followed saw a limited expansion of these sectors. It was only at the turn of the century that heavy industry grew at a fast rate, not least thanks to the introduction on a vast scale of hydro-electric power which offered a welcome solution to a country that lacked raw materials but had several waterways in the Alpine and Apennine regions. As one statesman, Francesco Saverio Nitti, emphatically remarked in 1905, the so-called 'white coal' would free Italy from a 'secular state of economic inferiority'. The first electricity companies were founded between 1884 and 1894 and by 1911 electrical power accounted for half of all industrial power.

Did Italy's first industrial take-off happen because of or in spite of economic protectionism? Historians and economists have long debated this issue. Some berated protectionism for establishing an immovable bloc of interests comprising large estate owners (wheat was one of the protected goods) and heavy industry at the expense of consumers. A more positive view maintained that Italy, like many latecomers, including Germany and Japan, managed to industrialize thanks to the introduction of tariffs on imported goods as well as State intervention in the economy. More recent interpretations have partially revised the overall importance of this issue in view of the relatively modest level of the tariffs imposed on foreign goods. Beyond these controversies, the role of the Liberal State in promoting industrialization has generally been viewed favourably. The promotion of transport and communications through railway and road construction, the provision of credit to industry, not least through the banking sector, and the development of the school system all contributed to the industrial spurt of the early 20th century.

The 1900s also saw the beginning of State intervention in the South with a view to promoting its industrialization. In 1904, Giolitti's government approved special legislative measures for Naples, later extended to Basilicata, Calabria, and the other provinces. Among these measures were the creation of a large steel plant at Bagnoli, near Naples, which became operative in 1909; a hydro-electric plant on the river Volturno, also inaugurated in 1909, followed by various other waterworks; various tariff exemptions, and special credit rates. This legislation followed a public debate around the so-called 'Southern Question', which can be dated back to the 1880s, and which revolved around the perceived backwardness of this region and its need to catch up with the more developed areas. For many intellectuals, State intervention was necessary to redress this divide and to supplement market forces. These measures, however, were not sufficient in reducing the economic gap between the two areas of the country which had become evident at the beginning of the 20th century.

State intervention in the economy was strengthened during the fascist period, when Italy experienced an uneven trend in economic terms. The 1920s was a period of expansion and growth but the country was badly hit by the 1929 world crisis, with many industries and banks facing collapse. The State came to the rescue with a series of measures widely considered to have been effective and destined to have a long-standing impact. In 1931, it set up the IMI (Istituto Mobiliare Italiano) giving it the task of funding the industrial sector in order to relieve ordinary banks of this responsibility. In 1933, the State created the IRI (Istituto per la Ricostruzione Industriale), which took over ownership of shares of most heavy industry from the banks. Thus Italy ended up with the largest public sector of all the industrialized countries, a trait that continued to mark its economy in the post-war period, when public enterprises played a major role in shaping the country's industrial planning and future development.

The golden age of the Italian economy

The post-war years marked a period of unprecedented expansion, with GDP growing at a rate of 5 per cent between 1951 and 1963, reaching a peak of 8 per cent in the years after 1957, known as the 'economic miracle'. This rapid growth was due to a combination of domestic and international factors. Among the former, we find renewed State intervention in the economy coupled with a dynamic and forward-looking managerial style in the public sector; diffused entrepreneurship and inventiveness on the part of a myriad of small family firms in the private sector; and new social values revolving around consumerism and upward social mobility.

The country's founding role in the European Economic Community in 1957 was perhaps the most important external factor in the country's rapid growth at that time, as it contributed to a very considerable growth in exports, especially in terms of manufactured goods. This was the time when the country became renowned all over the world for its 'Made in Italy' brand, especially in textile, clothing, shoe and leather manufacturing, furniture, and interior design. This period was also characterized by renewed and sustained public schemes aimed at promoting the industrialization of the South, overseen and funded by a special State organization, the Cassa per il Mezzogiorno.

One of the positive factors accounting for the country's economic success was State intervention in the economy. After the war, it took a distinctive form with the setting up of various State-holding companies. These were directed by the Ministry for State Holdings, created in 1956 and managed by a group of technocrats who had in some cases formed their experience in the public sector during the fascist regime. A typical example is Pasquale Saraceno, who during the 1930s had worked at the IRI and in 1946 started working at the newly formed Svimez, a State-funded public–private consortium for the development of the South. Another prominent public manager was Enrico Mattei, who in 1952 became president of the newly formed oil and gas public company, Ente nazionale idrocarburi (ENI). A charismatic figure, Mattei set out to establish an oil supply network as an alternative to the one controlled by the Anglo-American giants, which he dubbed the 'seven sisters'. His life and premature death in 1962, when his private jet exploded in unexplained circumstances, have since inspired numerous books and various works of fiction. Among these, a 1972 film by acclaimed director Francesco Rosi (*The Mattei Case*) and, more recently, a 2009 popular TV mini-series entitled *Enrico Mattei: The Man Who Looked to the Future*.

Enjoying close links with the dominant party in power, Christian Democracy (DC), these managers both shared and upheld a coherent approach to economic development. Their ethos combined a strong belief in the need for State and social planning as a correction to the free market and Catholic values based on class collaboration and solidarity. When the Socialist Party joined the coalition governments in the early 1960s, the prevailing strategy did not change; indeed there was a further impulse towards State intervention which led to the electrical sector being nationalized in 1962.

The role of State-owned enterprises was particularly decisive in promoting heavy industry, especially the engineering, metal, and chemical sectors, which were still considered to be of strategic importance to national interest. This also explains the trajectory taken by industrialization in the South, as it was the public sector that was responsible for the opening of new industrial plants in this area of the country, under the umbrella of the Cassa per il Mezzogiorno. Iron and steel plants, oil refineries, and petrochemical factories were set up in the southern regions, accounting for the majority of industrial jobs. However, they failed to stimulate the growth of related industries in the surrounding areas and ended up as isolated enclaves, which gained them the nickname of 'cathedrals in the desert' (Figure 5). The traditional sectors of manufacturing and tourism were, by contrast, neglected. Hence, while State intervention through the Cassa played a major role in narrowing the economic gap between North and South, it was unable to have a long-lasting effect, as we shall discuss later.

Alongside State intervention in the economy we need to consider the extraordinary growth of a dynamic manufacturing sector, which was export-orientated and revolved around a variety of consumer goods, especially leather and textiles, mechanical goods, ceramic tiles, jewellery, and light engineering. This new industrialization affected new regions of the country, especially the Veneto, Friuli-Venezia Giulia, Emilia-Romagna, Marche, and other central regions. The strong

5. The state-sponsored AlfaSud plant at Pomigliano D'Arco, near Naples, which produced the AlfaRomeo Alfasud models between 1971 and 1986.

features of this model of industrialization were a high degree of flexibility in the organization of production and the agglomeration of myriad specialized small firms in specific towns and villages—the so-called industrial districts. Not many people are aware, for instance, that 80 per cent of Italian ceramic tiles are manufactured by several hundred firms located in and around the town of Sassuolo, in Emilia-Romagna, an area whose growth began in the 1950s and which nowadays exports almost three-quarters of its production to world markets. Or that sportswear is concentrated in and around the town of Montebelluna, in Veneto, where the industry developed in the 1960s on the strength of an artisanal tradition going back to the 19th century. Firms operating in this area account for 65 per cent of the global production of ski boots, 80 per cent of the world production of football boots, and 60 per cent of all cycling shoes.

An effective combination of family ties, artisanal know-how, sheer hard work (critics also point to labour exploitation), inventiveness, and entrepreneurship accounted for the growth of these districts. Even when some individual firms managed to emerge as world leaders, as the Benetton knitwear and clothing company did in the 1970s and 1980s, they relied upon a local manufacturing tradition and local skilled labour, as well as individual creativity and flair. In the case of Benetton, it was the knitting designs of one of the founder siblings, Giuliana, which secured the early success of the firm.

One industry where Italy conquered the European market was domestic appliance manufacturing, especially refrigerators. In the 1960s, Italy became one of the largest producers of refrigerators in the world, coming third after the United States and Japan. Firms in this sector, such as Ariston, Ignis, and Indesit, also grew out of an earlier artisanal tradition and soon produced for the cheap end of the export market. Despite being cheap to purchase, Italian-made appliances relied on a combination of advanced technology, traditional materials, and innovative design, thus helping to establish the reputation of the 'Made in Italy' brand for the technological, stylistic, and aesthetic qualities of its products.

Creativity and innovativeness were not just the hallmarks of new self-made entrepreneurs, as they also marked the rise of a pioneering group of industrial designers employed by the more established private companies. An interesting example is that of the aeronautical company Piaggio, which, after the war, decided to engage in the production of motor scooters. It entrusted this task to one of its engineers, Corradino D'Ascanio, who until then had designed helicopters. In 1946, D'Ascanio developed the Vespa ('Wasp') scooter, which in the following decades became one of the greatest and most enduring successes of Italian manufacturing. Production soon escalated, with two million produced in 1960, four million in 1970, and over ten million in 1988. According to legend, the designer derived his ideas from the aeronautical industry and even used parts of a plane for his creation, so much so that the scooter's small wheels are supposed to have originated from an aircraft's small landing wheels. While the story is apocryphal, what is true is that D'Ascanio made a number of ingenious innovations, including easy access onto the bike for riders, especially if they wore skirts (notably women but also priests), the addition of a spare wheel, and protection from exposure to the dirty engine. On the strength of this invention Piaggio went on to produce the iconic and versatile Ape ('Bee'), a three-wheeled commercial vehicle, in 1948, and the 50cc Vespino, aimed at teenagers, in 1963.

In short, the golden age of the Italian economy was due to the positive interaction and synergy between different internal and external factors, while the private and the public sectors were each able to contribute to the overall expansion and to the reduction of territorial imbalances. However, a combination of domestic weaknesses and external economic threats began to emerge in subsequent decades, until the virtuous cycle of the 1950s and 1960s turned into a downward spiral in the 1990s.

Slowdown and possible decline

The pioneering role played by the public industrial sector did not last beyond the 1970s. Political criteria and considerations increasingly influenced the appointment of new managers, who were less capable than their predecessors and more inclined to use their influence in order to provide jobs for members of the political parties and resources for their increasingly expensive machineries, as well as favours to voters. Nepotistic practices and corruption became widespread, and contributed to the worsening performance of State-owned firms. Throughout the 1980s the centre-left governments took very few steps to address this situation, so much so that by 1991 the combined debts of two State-holding companies, EFIM (Ente per il Finanziamento dell'Industria Manifatturiera) and IRI, had managed to exceed 5 per cent of GDP.

At the end of the decade, therefore, the Italian model of 'State capitalism' was in a dire situation and obviously in need of reform. As for State-led development of the South, it went sour in the same period. Both the 1973 oil crisis and the overproduction of steel in Europe in the 1980s were to cause the closure of many industrial plants and the abandonment of the overall strategy, culminating with the folding of the Cassa in 1984 and an end in 1992 to all extraordinary intervention in the South.

Since then, territorial disparity has once again been on the increase. Neither the central nor the regional governments have been able to develop alternative, coherent approaches for the South, amid growing disillusionment with the entire concept of economic development or indeed modernization in this part of the country. The 1980s was also the decade when public debt increased exponentially, from under 60 per cent of GDP in 1980 to roughly 120 per cent in 1994, although this was only in part due to the deficits incurred by State-owned firms. Other factors led to this increase, including a rise in the prices of raw materials as well as wages, an expansion of public administration and employees, and a particularly generous pension system.

While the public sector became a burden for the State, the private sector, especially in the shape of small firms and 'industrial districts', continued to perform well throughout the 1980s and to increase its share of total employment, while the larger firms were shedding jobs. Indeed Italy stood out among the industrialized countries for the size of its small firms sector. In 1993, manufacturing firms with fewer than twenty employees accounted for 89.7 per cent of all firms and for 38.7 per cent of all employees, whereas large firms with more than 500 employees employed only 19 per cent of the workforce. However, during the 1990s many small exporting firms were caught seemingly unprepared by the process of economic globalization, increasingly exposed to competition with producers of cheap foreign goods from Asian countries, especially China, which specialized in the same range of consumer goods. As a result, after 1995, the share of Italian exports as a percentage of world exports started to fall.

In the face of these adversities, many northern self-employed people and small entrepreneurs operating in industrial districts became increasingly frustrated with the high levels of taxation, rigid labour laws, large public deficit, and underperformance of public administration. They signalled their grievances against the State by shifting their votes from the DC to the Northern League party in the first half of the 1990s. For the first time since the turn of the century, solidarity with the South was openly questioned, as this party campaigned for regional autonomy, a smaller State, and an end to subsidies and redistribution policies that favoured the poorer areas of the country. In 1996–9, the Northern League stepped up its anti-Rome propaganda by threatening secession.

Thus the 'Southern Question' was being rapidly replaced by a 'Northern Question', whereby the more affluent and economically developed area of the country sent a message to the political establishment that was both crude and simple: reform the State or we shall leave and form an independent entity. Concern for the territorial integrity of the country became widespread in those years as testified by the titles of numerous books by prominent intellectuals, many of whom prophesied an imminent break-up of the nation-state.

The unravelling of the economic system, therefore, went hand in hand with what was termed the fiscal crisis of the Italian State and with the collapse of the First Republic political parties in 1992. This in turn opened the way for a profound re-adjustment of the Italian economy, not least as a result of pressure from the European Union, which had enshrined fiscal responsibility in the 1992 Maastricht Treaty and also established a Stability and Growth Pact in order to rein in the excessive debts of member states. Then in 1999, Italy joined the European Monetary Union and adopted the euro. Hailed as a success by policy-makers and the public alike, Italy's entry into monetary union helped stabilize its debt in spite of price rises in the short term. However, it also prevented the country from devaluing its currency in order to boost exports and stimulate growth.

Since then, successive governments have had to implement painful neo-liberal reforms, with uneven efforts and mixed results—privatizations, deregulation, cuts to public expenditure (especially to the generous pension system), and reform of the labour market to increase flexibility and reduce labour protection. These reforms aggravated the gap between older workers, who remain fairly well protected, and young people who struggle to find employment other than on a temporary basis.

Domestic opposition from a variety of entrenched interests and ideological opposition from right and left parties have limited the effectiveness of the various reforms which have been implemented. Furthermore, there are many who argue that these types of reforms have succeeded in dismantling the mixed public-private economic system which had underpinned Italy's extraordinary growth in the golden years but failed to replace it with a coherent alternative model. In this context, the slow pace of growth achieved in the 2000s and the recession of the early 2010s are seen as evidence that these reforms are not working and that the country will never recover lost ground. For some, it has embarked on a slow yet irreversible decline, while others see exit from the Eurozone as the only possible remedy.

Another area which successive governments have struggled to address is that of the large size of the black, or shadow, economy, estimated at around 20 per cent of GDP, and of the activities of organized crime groups, which account for roughly 10 per cent of GDP. While traditionally the Sicilian Mafia, the Neapolitan Camorra, and the Calabrian 'Ndrangheta specialized in fraud, extortion, and drug and cigarette smuggling, in recent decades they have successfully evolved into global syndicates and invested heavily in commercial and financial activities across Europe. In Italy itself, during the recession, organized crime groups were able to increase their stranglehold over sectors of the legal economy.

Fighting back

In 2015, Italy came out of recession, even though growth remained very limited. The real question is whether the country's economy in the last twenty years has been able to restructure and adjust to globalization or whether it is no longer able to compete in the international markets, despite the various attempts at reforms. To address this question, we need to revisit the main pillars of the economy—the public sector, the large private firms, and the small firms prevalent in various industrial districts.

As concerns the public sector, privatizations were carried out in the 1990s and 2000s, leading to a reduction in the number and size of State enterprises. However, this process lacked impetus, in the absence of an appetite for neo-liberal reforms among the public and policy-makers, amid concerns that strategic sectors might end up under foreign control. Hence the State often retained a majority share in partially privatized companies. Local public services, on the other hand, have not been privatized to any significant degree, partly because of public opposition and partly because local governments often see them as an important instrument for exercising influence (and patronage). A half-hearted policy of deregulation was implemented piecemeal, with the result that economic competition in transport, telecommunications, the energy sector, and the liberal professions has increased only at a modest pace. Public administration was also reformed and bureaucracy simplified, although arguably still leaving much scope for improvement.

One significant recent trend that has accompanied these reforms has been a shift in power from local and regional governments towards the central State, despite successive reforms aimed at decentralization and regional autonomy implemented in the 2000s. This shift has brought to light a fundamental tension between the different tiers of government, with local and especially regional governments resisting cuts to expenditure and the central government keen to offload the burden of austerity measures onto the lower tiers. There are also regional imbalances, as per-capita expenditure varies greatly across the national territory. In 2010, it amounted to just over 2,200 euros in Lombardy as opposed to over 13,000 euros in Valle D'Aosta and 5,350 in Sicily. Valle D'Aosta and Sicily are two of the five regions enjoying a special statute (hence enhanced autonomy). Together with Trentino Alto-Adige, Friuli Venezia-Giulia, and Sardinia, they are the highest spenders.

If change in the public sector has been uneven and at times contradictory, not least because of a lack of drive and conviction among both policy-makers and Italian public opinion as far as neo-liberal reforms are concerned, the large private firms have also been slow in adapting to change. According to a recent interpretation (Catani 2014), large public and private enterprises suffer from common weaknesses, notably an old-fashioned corporate governance; a lack of turnover at managerial levels, with most executives over the age of 70; a complete lack of diversity given the overwhelming white male profile, with few women managers and even fewer foreigners; and the dominance of family values. These features hinder the internationalization of Italian firms, which in turn impacts on their ability to compete in the global market.

One success story, albeit a very controversial one, has been that of the historic car-manufacturing firm, Fiat, owned by the Agnelli family. Already an important company during the first spurt of industrialization, it grew to dominate the domestic mass market in the 1950s and 1960s, helped by the State's construction of public motorways, starting with the A1, the so-called Autostrada del Sole (Motorway of the Sun), which was opened in 1964. In

2004, after several years of struggling with loss of profitability and market share, the Agnelli family appointed as CEO Sergio Marchionne, who was born in Italy but whose family had migrated to Canada when he was aged 14. In 2008, Marchionne rescued the company and internationalized it through the acquisition of the American firm Chrysler, then facing bankruptcy.

The resulting Fiat Chrysler Automobile (FCA) has since gone from strength to strength. Marchionne was accused in Italy of deliberately pursuing an abrasive and confrontational style—he laid off hundreds of managers and took on the powerful metal-mechanical trade unions—and of neglecting Fiat's long-standing links with Turin as well as the debt it owed the Italian State. In 2014, in fact, Fiat decided to move its legal headquarters to the Netherlands and its fiscal headquarters to Britain. However, Marchionne promised not to close down factories operating in Italy and to re-employ thousands of workers who had been temporarily laid off. Nevertheless, the number of cars and trucks actually produced in Italy declined drastically, from 1.7 million in 2000 to less than 700,000 in 2012.

In 2015, Fiat announced that it planned to add more than 1,000 new workers at its Melfi plant in southern Italy. Later that year, FCA relaunched the iconic Alfa Romeo brand when it unveiled the new Alfa Romeo Giulia in a highly choreographic show. On that occasion, Marchionne stated that the new car was only the beginning of an 'aggressive production plan' which envisaged the sale of seven million automobiles by 2018, against the 4.4 million sold in 2014. Despite its achievements, it is doubtful whether the strategy undertaken by Fiat will be followed by other large firms. It is certainly at odds with Italian industrial practice and ethos, and may entail too much social confrontation to be adopted on a large scale.

Finally, the small firms sector has proved to be much more resilient than it was expected to be in the 1990s, when the industrial districts' success story gave way to pessimistic tales of de-industrialization and slow death. Despite the small size of many firms, some industrial districts relocated parts of their production abroad but also managed to retain most of their strategic operations. Others increasingly relied on migrant labour. Admittedly, some did struggle, and others succumbed and disappeared altogether. Nevertheless, in 2015, the Italian industrial districts managed to return to their 2008 level of turnover and to their traditional leading role in exports. Furthermore, the average size of firms had increased, while foreign companies had invested and made acquisitions in a number of districts.

As at the height of the economic boom, the most successful companies are those which blend new technology with traditional methods and occupy niche positions. One firm epitomizing this is Fazioli, established in 1981 by an engineer-cum-pianist with a passion for producing pianos with a uniquely 'Italian' sound. Combining his own expertise with that of his parents' furniture-making business, Paolo Fazioli created the instruments by making use of the same type of wood that was used originally to produce Stradivarius violins. The hand-made pianos have since become the preferred choice of many prominent professional artists, so much so that all but a few of the 130 instruments produced each year are exported worldwide.

In short, catastrophic forecasts of the collapse of the economy are misguided, as Italy maintains some important features of strength. Low value-added production has been phased out due to cheap competition from abroad, yet Italian manufacturers have remained competitive at the higher end of the market, where the price level does not deter consumers whose focus is on the aesthetic and quality value of the products. Hence the 'Made in Italy' brand remains strong and attractive, not least in Asian countries, where higher standards of living have led to growing imports of luxury goods. Italian companies are being bought by external buyers, as foreign investment is on the rise. Industrial districts have defied gloomy predictions and regained their competitiveness, albeit having gone through a painful restructuring. However, territorial imbalances continue to weigh heavily on the country's future prospects. As revealed in 2015 by an official report, in the period 2001–14 GDP in the South had fallen by 9.4 per cent while it had grown by 1.5 per cent in the rest of the country.

The last twenty years, therefore, have left behind a mixed record. There is no doubt that membership of the Eurozone opened a new, difficult phase for the Italian economy, especially given the high exchange rate of the new currency. A series of neo-liberal reforms aimed at reducing public expenditure and kick-starting growth, like increasing labour market flexibility, selling off State enterprises and streamlining bureaucracy, was implemented by successive governments, albeit only half-heartedly. The role of the State in the economy, in particular, hangs in the balance, as many remain convinced that public enterprises are still of national strategic importance and that overall control should not be ceded to the private sector.

Membership of the euro has provided Italy with a package of measures it needs to implement in order to restructure its economy and achieve long-lasting stability and growth. However several years of slowdown have greatly impaired Italian people's trust in the medicine they have been prescribed and even in the doctor. The result is that one of the strongest and longer lasting myths in the history of Italy since the Unification—that of Europe as a positive modernizing force—has been seriously weakened. As with the standard of living of the Italian people, therefore, the preservation of the 'European dream' may hinge on a sustained recovery of the economy.

Chapter 5
Emigration, immigration, and citizenship

In the 19th and 20th centuries, Italy experienced massive rates of emigration, primarily from the southern regions but also from the poorer areas of the North, especially from the Veneto, the same region which from the 1960s became the epicentre of the small-scale model of industrialization. Mass emigration contributed to rising levels of consumption at home thanks to the emigrants' remittances to their families but was also a source of humiliation to national pride.

Internal migration also reached high levels, in line with industrialization and urbanization. For many decades it was predominantly a local phenomenon, but in the 1960s it took on the form of long-distance migration from the South to the North, generating social and housing problems and, above all, cultural prejudices—even quasi-racist attitudes of rejection—on the part of many northern residents. Yet in the longer term this massive dislocation of people from one end of the peninsula to the other contributed to cementing that often elusive public good—a shared sense of nationhood—not least when coupled with the effects of mass consumerism and television.

When Italy started to become the chosen destination for foreign migrants in the 1970s there were those who believed that due to its own past as a country of emigrants it would be more sympathetic to their plight and more prone to show solidarity towards the newcomers than other advanced countries had proved to be. This did not turn out to be the case—perhaps because the experience of Italian emigrants abroad had not been properly debated and integrated into a national narrative. After an initial period in which the phenomenon went largely unacknowledged, in the 1990s the Northern League started to campaign on an anti-immigrant platform, evoking strong images of 'hordes of foreigners' invading the country and threatening the Italian way of life and well-being. The electoral success of this party and its participation in successive governments headed by Berlusconi then placed the 'immigrant question' at the top of the list of concerns affecting Italians (until it was displaced by economic issues in later years).

Emigration and immigration have both impacted on Italy's approach to citizenship, which is based on *jus sanguinis* (ancestry), as opposed to *jus soli* (place of birth). Indeed the former has been interpreted in a very generous manner, partly to offer a form of redress to all those Italians who had to leave their homeland, thus making it relatively easy for citizens of other countries such as Brazil and Argentina to acquire Italian nationality if they can claim to be of Italian descent. By contrast children of migrants born in Italy, attending Italian schools, and speaking the language on an everyday basis are not granted citizenship until they reach the age of 18, and even then they do not acquire it automatically. While most political parties are aware that this situation is unsustainable, they have so far been unable to counteract Northern League rhetoric which denies that immigrants are in Italy to stay or that the country has become multicultural. A serious debate on what it means to be Italian in ways that embrace ethnic and cultural diversity has not yet been attempted.

However, there are signs of change. In 2013, the new centre-left government signalled its intention to turn a new page by appointing Cécile Kyenge, of African descent, as minister for integration and the country's first black minister. In 2014, Prime Minister Renzi promised to make it easier for migrants' children to become Italian citizens. While public policies aimed at integration have been lagging behind, there has been much significant development at social and cultural levels, with a rapid increase in the number of migrants turned entrepreneurs, a growing contribution of migrants to cultural production, including literature, music, and cinema, a rise in inter-ethnic marriages, and a considerable presence of second-generation migrants who have mobilized themselves in order to promote a reform of the country's citizenship laws.

Emigration

The history of modern Italy, like that of Ireland, has been characterized by mass emigration. Between 1861 and 1990, more than twenty-eight million Italians left their country, a figure slightly higher than the entire population of the newly formed nation-state. The vast majority emigrated for economic reasons, especially due to poverty levels and a lack of opportunities at home. Contrary to common perceptions, the North contributed substantially to this haemorrhage of people, especially up to the First World War. Not surprisingly, as Italy's first spurt of industrialization affected primarily the north-western regions, it was the north-east, particularly Veneto, which accounted for the highest outflows. It was only in the 20th century that emigration from the South became dominant. In both cases the emigrants were mainly male, unskilled, and from rural areas, and they intended to return home after a few years to acquire their own plot of land. Indeed, many did manage to return after accumulating a certain amount of money. After the First World War, however, the number of women emigrating started to rise, as they joined their husbands and sons to settle permanently abroad.

While the reasons for emigrating and the composition of the migrants were similar across Italy, the countries of destination were markedly different, especially before 1945. Most northern Italians migrated to European countries, often on a seasonal basis given the geographical proximity to France, Germany, and Switzerland. Southern Italians, on the other hand, tended to go to the United States, Latin America, and Australia. In the 1950s and 1960s, external migration was primarily to Europe, while internal migration flows from the South to the North, and north-east to north-west, further contributed to the massive scale of population transfer. Roughly 1.5 million people moved every year between 1951 and 1965.

Mass emigration had several economic, social, and cultural consequences as well as, arguably, important political ones too, the legacy of which is still relevant today. In economic terms, the money the emigrants were able to send back to relatives at home contributed both to a rise in the standards of living of many families and to a positive balance of payments. This was especially the case in the early 20th century and after 1945. More widely, millions of Italians living abroad contributed to the creation of a mass market for national products, initially food and wines but later fashion and design too. Thus the 'Made in Italy' brand owes a considerable part of its success to the continuing exodus of the country's citizens.

In social and cultural terms, emigration had enduring consequences. For the migrants themselves, it often involved hardship, exploitation, and discrimination in the countries where they settled. This was mainly the case before the Second World War. Migrants tended to establish 'Little Italies' abroad, and, especially in the United States, they were perceived collectively as inferior, untrustworthy, and of criminal tendencies. It is ironic that in North America, Italian food was generally snubbed as unhealthy, in view of the complete reversal of fortune that it underwent from the 1920s onwards.

Paradoxically, these attitudes, as well as the novel experience of living side by side with fellow citizens originating from different parts of Italy, promoted among Italian migrants a sense of national identity, even if it did not completely supplant their previous local allegiances. Among the women who stayed at home, there developed a parallel growth in awareness of the Italian nation-state, as many had to deal with bureaucratic practices and/ or make demands on the municipal and State agencies on behalf of themselves and their absent male relatives. With time, however, individual allegiances shifted to the countries of settlement as these Italians became successfully assimilated. Nowadays, Italian-Americans have fully integrated in and are considered an asset for the USA; and in Argentina people of Italian origin make up roughly 50 per cent of the population.

The attitude of the Italian State towards emigration during the Liberal phase was ambivalent. On the one hand, successive governments attempted to regulate and control a phenomenon which was perceived as damaging to society and even shameful to a State aspiring to become a European power. On the other hand, policy-makers viewed emigration as an asset and pursued a policy of cultural penetration among migrant communities, opening up Italian schools, celebrating national festivities, and fostering feelings of attachment to the homeland. At the beginning of the 20th century, the rise of a radical form of nationalism led many intellectuals to reconcile their expansionist and bellicose ideas with the need to find an outlet for Italian emigrants by advocating the conquests of colonies in Africa. When Mussolini came to power, initially he adopted a tolerant attitude towards emigration but later considered it detrimental to the reputation of the fascist regime and sought to prevent Italians moving abroad unless they went to the colonies. He also established new laws preventing people from moving internally from rural to urban areas, in line with the regime's idealization of pastoral life and values.

After 1945, the governments removed both internal and external barriers and emigration, both European and transoceanic, resumed at a fast pace, until it started to decrease in the 1970s.

The long-standing policy of fostering cultural and economic links with migrant communities (significantly referred to as 'Italians abroad') was also rediscovered. Since the 1990s, Italy's sluggish economic growth has led to rising rates of emigration, this time especially among highly skilled and well educated young people, creating a worrying 'brain drain'.

Despite the obvious attempts by different governments to pursue expansionist policies abroad through strengthening migrants' links with their homeland, numerous scholars have highlighted the curious absence of the issue and theme of emigration in official commemorative practices, in school textbooks, and among society at large. It was only in 2009, for instance, that the first national museum of emigration was opened in Rome. Albeit belatedly, the decision to house it at the Vittoriano (the 'Altar of the Fatherland') clearly marked an intention to inscribe mass emigration into the national narrative at the highest level. As the then undersecretary for foreign affairs, Alfredo Mantica, stated, 'The aim of the museum is to reinstate in the history of Italy a story that is often little known or which tends to be considered of an inferior level'.

Why it should have taken so long to officially commemorate this aspect of the nation's past is an interesting question. State shame and guilt at not being able to prevent the massive exodus of Italians probably played a part. The internal population move from the South to the North in the post-war decades, and the prejudices and discrimination encountered by the migrants in the northern cities, where they were often denied the status of 'fellow citizen', may also have contributed to the difficulty of telling a wider story about migration. This raises the related important issue of how the story is told to and/or received by the public now, as it may build a bridge towards integrating the migrants who have settled in Italy in the last few decades; or it may be framed in terms of redressing the plight of Italian migrants abroad while reinforcing the idea of blood ancestry. In either case, there are clear implications for Italy's citizenship policies, as will be discussed further in this chapter.

Immigration

In the 1970s, the rate of emigration started to decrease significantly, and instead Italy became a country of immigration. The phenomenon went largely unnoticed for almost two decades, due both to the relatively low numbers of incomers, and to the strong female as well as Catholic composition of the immigrants. The high female presence, which continues to this day, can be accounted for by a growing demand on the part of Italian families for domestic workers and carers for their children and the elderly, given both the traditional reliance on home-based care for the aged and the limited provision of public services in these areas. These workers tended to form an almost invisible workforce, and were generally perceived as performing socially useful tasks while not constituting a threat to law and order.

In 1991, the number of foreigners living in Italy still amounted to less than a million. In 2015, however, it had risen fivefold, with just over five million people of non-Italian origin living in the country—roughly 8.5 per cent of the population. By then, immigration had come to be considered a serious problem rather than being beneficial, despite repeated warnings from demographic experts that the ageing population of Italy was growing, due to the country's very low fertility rate and inhabitants' rising life expectancy, and that this could only be counteracted by massive inflows of young migrants. Various surveys carried out in the 2000s showed that the Italian public scored very highly in expressing concern about the levels of immigration to their country and viewing the phenomenon as presenting a very big problem.

The dramatic change in the way in which Italians reacted to immigration, from a prevailing attitude of largely ignoring the phenomenon to construing it in almost exclusively negative terms, can be attributed to a variety of factors. Among these, highly politicized and stereotypical portrayals of migrants as posing a threat to the 'Italian' way of life have come to play an increasingly important role, spearheaded by the Northern League party. Other reasons have less to do with representations of migrants and more to do with the characteristics of these migration flows and (lack of) official regulatory policies. For example, the make-up of the migrant population has been very heterogeneous, as Italy, unlike other European countries, has lacked a steady and regulated inflow from former colonies. It has had a high incidence of 'illegal', undocumented migrants who have ended up working in the shadow economy and/or surviving on petty crimes, which has in turn reinforced negative perceptions of 'foreigners' as contributing to rising levels of criminality. And, finally, the manner in which immigration into Italy has developed has been largely unplanned and spontaneous, with successive governments reacting to the situation ex-post rather than developing proactive policies.

Migrants have reached Italy from a wide variety of countries. In the 1990s, most migrants came from North Africa as well as from the Philippines. Later, they originated mainly from Eastern Europe, Asia, and Latin America. Between 2006 and 2007, when Romania joined the EU, Italy became the preferred destination for its migrants, and today there are over one million Romanians there, constituting the largest minority group in the country. Apart from working for Italian families and in the informal economy, many found stable employment in the myriad small and medium-sized firms in the north-eastern and central regions of Italy. There they tended to carry out the least skilled jobs, helping many firms keep production at home rather than outsourcing it to countries with lower labour costs, which has in turn contributed in no small manner to the well-being of the local economy.

However, the traditionally tight-knit, family-based, and cohesive nature of the industrial model prevalent in these areas has resulted in higher than average levels of concern for and even rejection of the migrant presence. As such, wide acknowledgment of the economic benefits brought by immigration to the region has gone hand-in-hand with fear of the long-term cultural and social consequences of the mass influx of 'foreigners'. These contradictory attitudes have in turn been exploited and exacerbated by the radical, xenophobic political stance of the Northern League party. By contrast, Catholic organizations have been at the forefront of providing services and assistance to these migrants and in advocating social solidarity.

The Italian governments' approach to immigration has proved to be in line with the prevailing public reaction and party stances. In the 1990s, legislation approved by centre-left coalitions dealt with the phenomenon from the perspective of integrating the new migrants into society. The 1998 Turco–Napolitano law, in particular, was inspired by the belief that immigration, contrary to early expectations, had taken on a permanent nature and required both regulatory and integration policies, as well as a reform of the country's citizenship rules. The law aimed at granting migrants access to jobs and social rights but it also linked the approval of visas to work permits and introduced Centres of Temporary Stay where migrants were to be detained for up to thirty days for administrative purposes.

By then, however, the issue had become heavily politicized, so much so that the centre-right launched a campaign of intransigent opposition to the new legislation, vowing to repeal it once in government. In 2002, the newly formed Berlusconi government introduced a new law—the so-called Bossi–Fini law—which was deliberately presented and popularized as draconian, even though it largely retained the already existing norms. However, the rhetoric accompanying the approval of the new legislation was especially unwelcoming for migrants. In particular, it raised the spectre of a cultural clash between a 'Christian' model of society, based on traditional values that had to be preserved and

6. **Northern League 2008 election poster depicting an American Indian with the slogan 'They suffered immigration. Now they live in reserves'.**

protected, and a 'universal multiracial' model that was to be rejected and resisted (Figure 6).

In 2008, another Berlusconi government approved a new series of highly controversial measures, dubbed the 'security package', which for the first time introduced the 'crime of clandestinity', establishing that undocumented migrants would be punished with a fine and even a period of imprisonment. Quite apart from widespread condemnation by organizations such as Amnesty International, the new law was considered inapplicable by many experts. The apparent contradiction between the draconian content of the law and the unlikelihood for it to be enforceable can be explained by the fact that much of the new legislation aimed primarily at reassuring the public that law and order and the phenomenon of 'clandestine immigration' were a government priority.

Nevertheless, the legislation approved in the 2000s had the combined effect of exacerbating the precarious status of many migrants and making their integration into Italian society yet more difficult. Furthermore, it connived with the public's explicit desire to drastically curb the number of migrants, rather than officially acknowledging the need for, and benefits of, inward migration. Nonetheless, in practice, the Berlusconi governments followed in the footsteps of previous legislators in introducing amnesties for illegal immigrants, hence implicitly recognizing that the vast majority of them were in Italy to live and work, and could not be sent back to their countries of origin. As for migrants attempting to reach Italy across the Mediterranean, however, the Berlusconi government followed a policy of intercepting and sending back to Libya any boats that were intercepted at sea, following an agreement between the two countries signed in 2008.

The return of centre-left governments in 2013 heralded the launch of an internationally much acclaimed rescue operation, known as 'Mare Nostrum'. This was approved by Prime Minister Enrico Letta following the death of 366 migrants in a shipwreck off the coast of Lampedusa, the Italian island in the middle of the Mediterranean which in the last few decades has been one of the targeted destinations for Africans escaping poverty, persecution, and bloody conflicts. The operation saved thousands of lives and was praised by migrant welfare organizations. With the costs of the operation escalating and criticisms from the right increasing, however, there were repeated calls for the government to involve the rest of the EU. However, as Letta himself recalled in 2015, despite his asking the EU to make a concerted effort to intervene, 'in the end the burden remained entirely on Italy's shoulders'.

Finally, in 2014, Prime Minister Matteo Renzi succeeded in convincing the EU to replace Mare Nostrum with Operation Triton, albeit with less than a third of the funding previously provided by Italy. Not surprisingly, the number of shipwrecks and deaths at sea increased very significantly after the folding of Mare Nostrum, until in April 2015 the EU decided to treble the funds for its own search and rescue operation. In the ensuing months,

Italian coast guards stepped up their rescue missions in the Mediterranean in the face of record numbers of people attempting the crossing from northern Africa.

In short, Italy has been in the spotlight for both discriminating against migrants at home and for saving their lives at sea, which highlights the country's difficulty in negotiating a consensual approach to immigration. This in turn reflects a deep-seated reluctance to accept and promote Italian society as pluralistic, diverse, and multi-ethnic, although attitudes have recently started to shift.

Citizenship

During the Risorgimento the Italian nation was conceived in ethnic and kinship terms, and since then the prevailing approach to citizenship has been based upon family descent. Traditionally, it was only through male ancestry that the newborn could become an Italian citizen. However, in 1948, a specific ruling by the new Constitutional Court established that women as well as men could pass on their citizenship. These norms also applied to Italians who had emigrated abroad. Indeed the country's legislators have been fairly relaxed in granting citizenship even to descendants of Italians, specifically to those whose paternal or maternal grandparent had been born in Italy and had not voluntarily renounced his/her citizenship rights. In recent decades, various regional governments have made explicit attempts to attract and facilitate the return of local migrants' descendants as a way of addressing the problem of the ageing population, and in the often mistaken belief that these individuals would integrate more easily into Italian society than immigrants without blood ancestry. Between 1998 and 2010, one million people of Italian descent successfully obtained Italian citizenship through their consulate—the vast majority from Latin America, and roughly a tenth from Australia, Canada, and the United States.

The concept of 'Italians abroad' has also inspired a favourable approach towards granting political and voting rights to Italians who emigrated abroad. After the Second World War this policy was advocated mainly by the nationalist and neo-fascist party, the Movimento Sociale Italiano. When the party turned into the National Alliance (AN) in 1995 and joined the governments headed by Silvio Berlusconi, it was finally able to sponsor a new law which in 2001 granted voting rights to Italian citizens abroad. From then on the latter were able to register with their consulate and elect twelve deputies and six senators to the Italian Parliament. The proposer of the measure, MP Mirko Tremaglia, referred to it as a 'great reform of exceptional value', for reasons related to justice and democracy as well as for putting an end to 'a discrimination against millions of citizens who are part of the Italian system'. It was somewhat ironic that in April 2006, at the first national political elections in which Italian expatriates exercised their voting rights, they turned out to be decisive in electing the centre-left coalition, thus raising wider questions concerning the legitimacy of the whole process.

While the Berlusconi governments were not prepared to extend voting rights to immigrants living and working in Italy, the centre-left governments repeatedly contemplated this possibility but did not bring the required legislation to completion. This was also the case regarding citizenship, as Italy has proved as harsh to its immigrants as it has been generous with its emigrants. The former, in fact, need to be resident in Italy for ten years before they can apply to become Italian citizens and their children, currently numbering over a million, in turn, have to wait until they turn 18.

In 2014, Prime Minister Renzi announced that he would change the law, partly in response to the mobilization of migrants themselves, with the support of civil society organizations, in a national campaign for a reform of citizenship and voting rights. A few MPs from ethnic minorities have championed this cause

7. Cécile Kyenge, minister for integration in 2013–14, takes part in the campaign, 'I too am Italy', aimed at changing the country's citizenship laws. The campaign was launched on the 150th anniversary of the Italian Unification.

and kept the issue in the public domain. The most prominent was Cécile Kyenge, minister of integration in 2013. Despite often being subjected to ridicule and even openly racist slants, she bravely insisted in portraying immigration in positive terms (Figure 7). As she openly stated, changing the citizenship law would significantly improve the lives of many migrants but it would also 'convey the message that immigration is not a danger to Italian society, but rather an opportunity'.

In October 2015, the Chamber of Deputies approved a new law, which granted citizenship to all migrants' children born in Italy (as previously mentioned, currently numbering over one million), provided one of their parents had been in possession of a regular residence permit for a minimum of five years. Also, children of migrants who had been born outside Italy would be able to obtain citizen status after completing at least five years of formal schooling in Italy.

Embracing a pluralistic conception of national identity and citizenship has proved difficult in other respects, too. Italian women had to wait until 1945 before they gained the right to vote and the 1970s before their status within the family was considered to be on a par with that of their husbands. While they do now have full access to education and work, their rates of participation in the labour market are still low by European standards. Italy has not yet had a woman as prime minister or head of state, although political parties have started to pay attention to female representation in Parliament and in government. At the 2013 elections, the percentage of women MPs increased from 20 per cent to 30 per cent, while Laura Boldrini became the third female ever to preside over the Chamber of Deputies. Furthermore, in 2014, Renzi's new cabinet achieved gender balance.

Prominent women in leading roles have included Emma Bonino, EU commissioner between 1994 and 1999; Susanna Camusso, the first woman elected general secretary of Italy's largest trade union, the CGIL, in 2010; Emma Marcegaglia, the first woman to be elected president of the employers' association, Confindustria, in 2008 and to be appointed president of the State-holding company ENI in 2014; and Federica Mogherini, appointed to the post of high representative of the European Union for foreign affairs and security policy (dubbed 'Lady Pesc') in November 2014. Despite these achievements, cultural representations of women continue to emphasize their role within the family as wives and mothers, while in the media and on TV they are often portrayed as the embodiment of male gratification. All this despite the fact that a mass feminist movement was developed successfully as far back as the 1970s and was at the forefront of a campaign for equal rights, divorce, and abortion.

Until 2016, Italy was the only major European country not to have granted civil union rights to gay and lesbian citizens, although in recent years various local mayors, notably those of Bologna, Milan, and Rome, have signalled their dissent by legalizing marriages which had taken place abroad—an illegal practice but also one that raised awareness of the issue. As in the case of the citizenship law concerning immigrants, various attempts by centre-left governments to grant legal and social rights to same-sex couples came to nothing, partly because of the explicit opposition of the Catholic Church.

The issue was once again in the spotlight in July 2015, when the European Court of Human Rights ruled that Italy was in violation of Article 8 of the European Convention, which establishes the right to respect for private and family life. Following in the wake of Catholic Ireland's historic vote in favour of gay marriages in May 2015, the ruling impressed a new urgency to legislative proposals on civil unions. Finally, on 25 February 2016, the Senate approved a diluted bill which recognized civil unions for same-sex couples but did not grant them (as previously envisaged) limited rights for the adoption of partners' biological children. The law came into force on 5 June 2016 (Figure 8).

Religious diversity is another contentious area, especially as regards Islam. In Italy, Muslims number over one and a half million, yet there are only a handful of official mosques as public and political resistance to building any new ones runs high. Fears of terrorist threats have exacerbated public suspicion of followers of the Islamic religion.

A changing society

Italy has become an increasingly multi-ethnic country but has found it difficult to acknowledge, represent, and give legal substance to this new reality. The lack of visibility and memorialization regarding its past as a country of emigration may

8. Rome Gay Pride, 2013. Banners list the countries where gay people can marry. The one in white at the front asks the question 'In Italy when?'

have contributed to lower than expected levels of compassion and empathy towards the new immigrants, as some have argued. Similarly, the continuing popularity of the myth of Italy as a benign and enlightened colonizing power in Africa, in spite of academic research proving the contrary, has prevented a public debate on both colonial and postcolonial relations. In this context, the constant flow of migrants and refugees coming in from North Africa across the Mediterranean, accompanied by feelings of having been abandoned by the EU in having to rescue and shelter them on Italian soil, have led to an increasing level of frustration mixed with fear on the part of the Italian public. The economic crisis of the last two decades, the politicization of the issue of immigration by xenophobic parties, and the often sensationalist media reports have also played a part in construing immigration as a problem and a threat.

As for civil rights, the Berlusconi-led coalitions campaigned explicitly for the defence of traditional family values, while the parties on the left have trodden with care, partly because they have always governed in coalition with Catholic parties. However, the attitude of the Catholic Church itself has recently shown signs of change, with Pope Francis signalling he would accept civil partnerships among same-sex couples (though not marriages), and advocating equal treatment for women and men at work.

In the meantime, Italian society has started to become much more diverse. Inter-ethnic couples, for instance, amounted to 58,000 in 1991 but rose to over 200,000 in 2005. By 2011, mixed families constituted 7.4 per cent of the total. While migrants tend to carry out the more menial jobs, which has a detrimental effect on their social status and integration, many of them have become successful entrepreneurs, with over half a million firms being owned by non-EU citizens in 2015. Migrants' children born in Italy show rates of participation in secondary schools almost on a par with Italian students, and, in particular, they have shown a propensity to shift from vocational to academic education and to go on to university, which may bode well for their future social mobility. Young migrants have also acquired a growing awareness of their hybrid identities and of the need to engage collectively in changing society. On the blog of the 'second generations', *Yalla Italia*, they introduce themselves by rejecting all current definitions, including 'immigrants' children' and 'new Italians', arguing that these expressions 'do not capture the dynamism and speed with which Italian society is changing' or indeed 'the real country'.

The greater diversity of Italian society has recently begun to affect media representations and public opinion. In November 2013, the pasta manufacturers Barilla publicly announced they would run a more inclusive and diverse ad campaign, after the company was threatened by boycotts following its chairman's assertion that he would never use a gay family in his adverts. Nine months later, frozen food company Findus launched the first ever ad on Italian

TV featuring a gay couple. Italian public opinion has shifted decisively in favour of both same-sex civil unions and a reforming of the citizenship law for migrants and their children.

Beyond the stances of the political parties and the media, therefore, it is within civil society that we find the best examples of active forms of citizenship and support for diversity, and it is in the everyday practices among, and exchanges between, children, youth, and ordinary working people that the foundations for a future, inclusive and integrated, new Italy are being built.

Chapter 6
Italy's 'soft' power

Italy has traditionally failed to influence the world through the use of 'hard' power, that is to say, through military and/or economic means. Its most notable attempt to do so during the fascist regime led to tragic outcomes. Since 1945, it has, however, accomplished the not inconsiderable task of seducing the world thanks to the 'soft' power of its culture and lifestyle. Soft power was defined by political scientist Joseph Nye as 'the ability to get the outcomes you want without having to force people to change their behaviour through threats or payments'. This was especially the case during the post-war period of industrialization, when the country almost effortlessly managed to surge to global popularity for its design, fashion, food, art, literature, and cinema.

Nowadays, the country's global reputation remains very strong, notwithstanding its recent economic decline, as Italy was ranked tenth in 2015 according to an international index of 'soft power'. This is due primarily to the enduring appeal of the 'Made in Italy' brand, which in turn relies on cultural (often also stereotypical) images, at times in contradiction with each other. Thus Italy exercises a strong attraction as an exotic land where it is still possible to enjoy a relaxed existence in idyllic rural retreats away from the frenetic lifestyle of the most advanced countries, but also as the epicentre of urban glamour, style, and fashion. For example, the cult Sicilian detective series featuring Inspector Montalbano,

9. Milan's fashion week, established in 1958 alongside those of London, New York, and Paris.

written by Andrea Camilleri and adapted for television, has successfully depicted the island as an alluring place where life (when not interrupted by murder) trundles along at a gentle pace and revolves around love, beauty, food, and wine against a backdrop of breathtaking sea and mountain views, and historic towns. Every year, on the other hand, Milan Fashion Week thrives upon glitz and luxury, celebrities, extensive partying, and flamboyant designers (Figure 9).

This chapter explores the various dimensions that make up Italy's soft power, including art and architecture, cinema, literature, gastronomy, fashion, and sport as well as diplomacy. It traces the rise of this power back to the intense creativity and innovativeness of the 1960s, 1970s, and 1980s. This was the period when Italian art and design successfully sustained and blended with business entrepreneurship and consumerism. On the other hand, however, within this sector there also developed an anti-market and anti-commercial strand, as with the highly influential avant-garde movement of the 1960s known as 'Arte Povera' ('Poor Art') that pioneered the use of everyday materials such as vegetables in its works.

Today we continue to see the impact of both strands of art and culture. Thus one strand of contemporary Italian architecture shuns grandiose projects in favour of more low-key, 'responsible' community projects. At the other end of the spectrum, renowned architects like Renzo Piano design buildings which are icons of advanced technology, and cities like Rome have been attempting to update their traditional cultural image by putting themselves forward as centres for 21st-century art. The critique of the ill effects of modernity has reverberated even within the more mundane sphere of gastronomy. The Slow Food movement, mentioned in the Introduction, was launched as a response to the sudden 'invasion' of the industrial fast food culture, promoting the idea that Italy and the world had to go local rather than global in food sourcing and distribution. However, the highly successful 'Eataly' chain, founded in 2007 by Oscar Farinetti, is fast becoming a global business, bringing Italian food to many corners of the world, with branches already opened in Dubai, Chicago, New York, Tokyo, São Paulo, and new ones planned in Moscow, London, and Paris.

Art and architecture

Building on the artistic and architectural movements of the first half of the 20th century, such as Futurism and Modernism, Italian creative art and design became internationally renowned in the post-war period thanks to a unique synergy between a new generation of industrial entrepreneurs and young designers and architects. The result was the reinvention of everyday domestic objects, especially lamps, chairs, tables, and kitchen utensils, as both functional and aesthetic items. The Arco lamp, designed in 1962 by Achille and Pier Giacomo Castiglioni, the sets of dining chairs by Giò Ponti (who also famously designed the Pirelli tower in Milan in the late 1950s), and the cocktail shaker designed by Luigi Massoni and Carlo Mazzeri in 1957 for the Alessi company are just a few examples of this new trend, known as 'bel design' or beautiful design.

In the late 1960s, in parallel with the growth of worker and protest movements, a new generation of radical architects and designers rejected the aesthetic approach linked to 'bel design' and developed a critique of both capitalism and consumerism. They created objects which provocatively combined rich and poor materials, deliberately distorted scale, and challenged traditional notions of style and beauty with kitsch designs. Yet some enterprising firms like Artemide went on to produce these creations and sell them to the public, while some of the radical designers themselves such as Ettore Sottsass Jr, founder of the Memphis group in the early 1980s, achieved international fame.

As mentioned earlier, it was in the late 1960s, too, that the avant-garde artistic movement known as Arte Povera developed in Italy, proving to be highly influential for many years to come. Its artists famously mixed poor organic materials with new technology, drawing attention to the devastating effects of modernization and consumerism. Arte Povera's most representative artist, Michelangelo Pistoletto, is especially known for his 'Venus of the Rags', first exhibited in 1967 and then re-made in different versions in subsequent years. In this striking artistic creation, a replica of the classical statue of Venus has her face almost buried in a pile of discarded clothes.

In 1972, the New York Museum of Modern Art (MoMA) pioneered an exhibition on Italian design, entitled 'Italy: The New Domestic Landscape'. As its curator, Emilio Ambasz, stated, the exhibition was organized in recognition of the fact that Italy 'is not only the dominant product design force in the world today but also illustrates some of the concerns of all industrial societies', among them 'a growing distrust of objects of consumption'.

Recently, in 2013, the Graham Foundation of Chicago re-presented the original MoMA exhibition both as a tribute to the long-lasting legacy of post-war Italian design and in order to promote a wider reassessment of the role and scope of architecture. In the meantime, the design objects created in the golden age of Italian industrialization have become highly sought after as collector items, with dedicated sales by the top international art galleries and auction houses. Similarly, Arte Povera has been revisited by various international exhibitions in recent years and its works have even started to appeal to global collectors.

Nowadays, it has become more difficult to speak of a specifically Italian design, as many Italian firms employ foreign designers and most architects work at an international level. Italy can boast world famous architects, part of the so-called 'archistars' set. The most renowned is Renzo Piano, together with Massimiliano Fuksas and Cino Zucchi. Piano rose to fame when he co-designed the Pompidou Centre in Paris in the 1970s, while in the 2000s he was responsible for the iconic Shard tower in London. After a decade of relative immobility on the architectural front during the 1990s, since the start of the 21st century various Italian city councils have commissioned prominent works and projects as part of an established trend to attract visitors—the so-called Bilbao effect, since that city renovated itself in 1997 thanks to its new Guggenheim museum designed by Frank Gehry—but also to demonstrate that the country was able once again to embrace change.

Turin, Milan, and Rome have been at the forefront of this process, but other cities have joined in. Indeed, Turin has successfully reinvented itself as a city of culture after the demise of Fiat by using the 2006 Winter Olympics as a springboard for launching a series of architectural projects, new museums, and new festivals. Rome itself commissioned various important buildings located away from the historic centre, among which the Museo Nazionale delle Arti del XXI Secolo, known as MAXXI, stands out as the first national museum for contemporary art in Italy. Designed by Baghdad-born, London-based Zaha Hadid, it sent the world the dual message that Rome should not be visited only for its past glories but also for its current status as a city that is ready to embrace foreign excellence and influence. Not far from the MAXXI, the Music Park designed by Renzo Piano has proved extremely popular with the public—hosting a variety of classical and popular music concerts, film and theatre shows, as well as cultural festivals and art exhibitions.

There is a growing realization that the post-industrial age requires a radically different and innovative approach to culture, including architecture, in order to revitalize local communities and promote development. This has recently led to various attempts to create 'cultural districts', building on the experience of Italy's famous 'industrial districts'. One successful example is that of the Langhe region, in Piedmont, where the economy previously revolved around the Ferrero manufacturing company renowned for its Nutella chocolate spread. Today the area has become a centre of tourist attraction thanks to its high-quality wine production of Barolo and Barbaresco and its traditional local food—this is the area where the idea of Slow Food originated—but thanks also to its new museums and visually striking 'green' architecture. In 2014, these wine-growing areas were included in the UNESCO World Heritage List, further boosting their global appeal.

Another example is that of the Val di Noto, in Sicily, also a UNESCO listed site since 2002 thanks to its unique baroque architecture. The area, which proudly defines itself as Italy's 'South-East' in contraposition to the manufacturing 'North-East', suddenly achieved worldwide fame thanks to the *Inspector Montalbano* TV series mentioned earlier, which are based on the popular Camilleri novels. The number of foreign visitors to the region has increased exponentially in recent years with dedicated 'Montalbano tours', and this in turn has led to the restoration of historic sites and a proliferation of cultural events.

At the political level, the strategy of using art and architecture as the springboard for economic recovery and international reputation has been embraced, albeit belatedly. The Renzi government in 2015 decided to target Italian museums, in the belief that they should offer visitors a wider experience than simply admiring works of art. It then proceeded to appoint various foreign directors to some of Italy's best known art galleries and archaeological sites, including the Uffizi in Florence. Culture Minister Dario Franceschini justified this controversial decision by stating that it represented a historic step towards the modernization of the Italian museum system. While many welcomed the attempt to aspire to global excellence in a field where Italy has obvious advantages over other countries, others criticized the growing commercialization of art and culture.

Italy today is also the home of young groups of architects like Tamassociati, winners of the 2014 Italian Architect Prize, who counter the glamour of the works of the 'archistars' by emphasizing the ethical and social dimension. Others have turned the spotlight on the impoverished urban suburbs and on the hundreds of unfinished mega-projects from past decades, which testify all over the country to the nefarious effects of political corruption and organized crime. Top of the list for the sheer number of derelict sites is Giarre, in Sicily, which a group of architects and artists recently proposed to transform into an archaeological and cultural site as witness to a dystopic age. Others still have focused on the pollution of the environment. For example, an itinerant exhibition by several artists in 2014, aimed at sensitizing public opinion, was inspired by the infamous Terra dei Fuochi ('Land of the Fires'), in Campania, used for decades as a dumping ground for toxic waste by the Camorra.

A recent encounter between different visions saw Renzo Piano—a life senator since 2013—collaborate with a group of young architects in small projects of urban regeneration in Turin, Rome, and Catania as a reminder and incentive to both the government and the public of the need to 'mend' Italian cities for their residents, rather than just making them visually attractive for foreign visitors. Named 'Periferie' ('Suburbs'), the overall project aims at addressing the issue of the outskirts, where huge residential developments were built quickly during the post-war boom, and which stand in stark contrast to the elegant historic centres.

Even veteran artists continue to promote an anti-consumerist message. Thus Arte Povera's Michelangelo Pistoletto, who was also active in the architectural field, founded the Cittadellarte Foundation in 1998, with the aim of promoting social inclusion and a sustainable environment, focusing on the re-use of the built heritage. In the 2000s, he went on to launch the 'Third Paradise' project, which set out to heal the fracture between the social and natural world. An example of his more recent art is the huge 'Reintegrated Apple', which first went on display in Milan's cathedral square in May 2015, symbolizing the need to repair our damaged earthly paradise.

Cinema, literature, and music

Italian cinema has made a huge contribution to the country's international image. In the post-war period, the neorealist movement, which showed the tragic impact of the war upon ordinary Italians as well as their everyday struggles and hardships during the reconstruction years, did much to attract sympathy to the country as well as to establish its long-lasting reputation for auteur directors, among them Vittorio De Sica, Federico Fellini, Roberto Rossellini, and Luchino Visconti. In parallel with this movement, the country developed a new genre, the so-called 'Commedia all'italiana' ('Italian-style comedy'), which appealed to popular audiences and often laid bare both Italians' worst traits and the country's most oppressive (and sexist) social customs. Thanks to these genres, Italian actors, both male and female, achieved stardom and were often in demand in Hollywood. In the 1960s, the genre known as 'spaghetti westerns' catapulted director

Sergio Leone, actor Clint Eastwood, and composer Ennio Morricone to global fame. Viewed at the time as just popular entertainment, these films have recently been re-evaluated for their highly innovative take on a traditionally American genre.

The fame of Italian cinema continued in the decades that followed with new auteur directors like Bernardo Bertolucci, Francesco Rosi, and later Nanni Moretti. An important new genre, which has emerged in the last two decades, deals with contemporary migration to Italy, exposing issues of exclusion and marginalization but also promoting dialogue and encounters between different cultures. Directors of both Italian and non-Italian origin, including Gianni Amelio, Matteo Garrone, and Ferzan Ozpetek, attempt to challenge the dominant stereotypical perceptions of migrants and present viewers with alternative portrayals of identity and belonging. Apart from these films, which are aimed at the more committed public, in recent times Italy has tended to produce popular (often low-quality) comedy films for internal consumption at one end, and auteur films for an external audience at the other, without being able to achieve a critical mass with a wide selection of middle-range products.

The country has tried to counter this situation by stepping up the organization of film festivals, with over 150 being held all over the peninsula every year. The one hosted by Venice is the oldest, as it was established in 1932; other major ones are held in Rome, Turin, Florence, Naples, Salerno, and Taormina. As well as vying with each other for hosting international cinematic events, Italian regions and cities have promoted themselves as film locations and even created new specialist centres since the demise in the 1970s of the famous Cinecittà film studios in Rome. Once known as the 'Hollywood on the Tiber', the latter complex has recently been revived thanks partly to subsidies offered to national and international companies, and partly to the creation of a cinema theme park with artworks designed by Dante Ferretti which opened in 2014.

Literary production seems to follow a different trajectory from cinema, as successive generations of novelists since the post-war period, many of them women, have succeeded in maintaining a high level of fiction in terms of both volume and quality, albeit against the backdrop of a dwindling domestic readership. However, only a few of them have appealed to an international audience, unlike earlier authors like Italo Calvino, Primo Levi, Elsa Morante, Alberto Moravia, Natalia Ginzburg, Cesare Pavese, and Leonardo Sciascia, to name just a few. The 1980s witnessed primarily the phenomenon of Umberto Eco's *Il nome della rosa* ('The Name of the Rose'), which was also turned into a successful film. In the 2000s, the novels by Alessandro Baricco and the non-fiction book *Gomorra* by Roberto Saviano were translated into English, the latter becoming an international bestseller as well as a popular film. An unlikely phenomenon characterizing the 2010s has been the international stardom achieved by an unknown novelist writing under the pseudonym of Elena Ferrante, whose four books set in the poorer districts of Naples and focusing on female friendship, violence, and rivalry have been acclaimed by the critics and become bestsellers around the world. Speculation as to the real identity of the writer has since been rife, but anonymity has so far been preserved.

Italy has also been able to rival other countries in the ever-popular crime fiction genre, with Gianrico Carofiglio, Michele Giuttari, and Massimo Carlotto joining the better known Andrea Camilleri in the list of writers appealing to an international audience. Italy's notoriety for corruption, intrigue, and organized crime also made it an ideal setting for numerous crime fiction series written by non-Italians, notably Michael Dibdin and Donna Leon. As in the case of cinema, recent literary production has included novels and stories written by migrants, some of whom, including Amara Lakhous, Younis Tawfik, and Ornela Vorpsi have achieved international recognition. Within Italy, various literary competitions reserved for migrant writers have contributed to raising their visibility among the public albeit at the risk of isolating them from the mainstream. The challenge for the future will be to avoid compartmentalizing such literature and focusing on widening the definition of what constitutes 'Italian' literature.

Together with art and architecture, throughout the centuries music has without doubt played a key role in fostering Italy's reputation abroad. Italian opera singers have often succeeded in appealing to the wider international public by focusing on popular arias and Neapolitan songs. While this was especially the case in the post-war period, the 1990s witnessed the remarkable rise to global fame of Luciano Pavarotti. He was admittedly helped by being heard singing the famous aria 'Nessun Dorma' from Puccini's opera *Turandot*, by several billion viewers all over the world during the 1990 World Cup tournament hosted by Italy. More recently, Andrea Bocelli has also achieved superstar status with a crossover between opera and pop music. Rising to popular fame is more difficult for classical musicians, yet this has been accomplished by a few Italian artists, most notably pianists and composers Ludovico Einaudi and Giovanni Allevi, both of whom developed original and hybrid styles. In 2015, Allevi was commissioned to compose a hymn ('O Generosa!') to be played at all official football championship matches. As the president of the Italian 'Serie A' league stated, 'The idea of composing a hymn for our matches arose from a desire to combine two pillars of Italian culture which we are famous for all over the world: our love for football, and our superb musical tradition'.

However, since the rise of modern styles like rock and pop, where the Italian language tends to act as a barrier rather than an asset, the country's artists have struggled to compete at an international level in these genres. From the late 1950s Italy saw the emergence of the so-called *cantautori*, or singer-songwriters who generally write both the text and the music of their songs. Generally considered high-quality artists, they became very popular in Italy and, in a few cases, abroad. One of the first *cantautori* was anarchist Fabrizio De André, roughly the Italian equivalent of Bob

Dylan in terms of both his reputation and the longevity of his fame. In a completely different style, Domenico Modugno became internationally known with his 1958 'Nel blu dipinto di blu' (better known as 'Volare'). Other prominent *cantautori* in the 1960s and 1970s included Francesco Guccini, Lucio Battisti, Edoardo Bennato, Lucio Dalla, and Pino Daniele. Vasco Rossi, Jovanotti Ligabue, and Gianna Nannini emerged in the 1980s, while Laura Pausini rose to fame in the 1990s, the latter two achieving international success.

In parallel with this phenomenon, in the 1970s, various Italian bands embraced progressive rock and went on to produce quality and unconventional music, among them Premiata Forneria Marconi, Banco del Mutuo Soccorso, and Le Orme. One genre for which Italy is appreciated abroad, and not least in the USA itself, is jazz, with several artists achieving recognition and one of the world's most important festivals being held in Umbria every summer since 1973. Nowadays the Italian musical scene has become ever more diverse. While the melodic and more conventional tradition continues to dominate the mainstream market but does not travel well abroad, there is a lively presence of indie artists and bands, some of whom have started to make inroads outside the country.

Food and wine

The global reputation and consumption of Italian food and wine have grown enormously in recent decades, bucking the more negative trend marked by other manufactured products. Italy's primacy stems from the vast diversity of its eno-gastronomic offer, a growing awareness of a healthy diet on the part of consumers, and the successful marketing of authentic flavours and artisanal traditions linked to different areas and regions, backed by certified labels. In addition, the popularity in both the UK and the USA of TV shows dedicated to Italian cuisine as well as travel books and novels recounting the experiences of American, British, and Canadian families in sharing the Italian (mainly Tuscan) way of life, have contributed to the country's international (and romanticized) appeal. One of the best known is *Under the Tuscan Sun*, published in 1996 by Frances Mayes and turned into a popular film in 2003.

A new strategy of focusing on quality and excellence has characterized the country's approach to its agricultural production in recent decades. This trend is especially marked in the wine industry, given that Italy used to produce mainly cheap bulk and table wines. This was especially the case in the southern regions and in Sicily. Starting in the 1980s, an impressive process of innovation, experimentation, and attention to indigenous varieties (Italy has the largest number of indigenous grape varieties in the world) led to the country's emergence as a leading producer and exporter of bottled wines. This was helped by the introduction of official wine classifications in the 1960s, with the DOC and DOCG quality assurance labels introduced in 1963 and the IGT label following in the early 1990s. For once this success story has involved the entire peninsula. Nowadays, in fact, the South has a growing number of acknowledged high-quality wines and is at the forefront in the campaign to revive traditional undocumented varieties originating in Greek and Roman times. Indeed Sicily has undergone a complete turnaround in its approach to wine-making and is currently one of the top Italian regions in terms of quality production.

The strategy of focusing on quality has clearly paid off. Italy today is the second country in the world after Spain for volume of exports and the second after France in terms of sales value. Its prosecco even surpassed champagne sales in 2013, becoming the world's most popular sparkling wine. In 2015, Italian producer Ferrari was awarded the trophy for Sparkling Wine Producer of the Year in the Champagne and Sparkling Wine World Championships in recognition that its classically produced wines were able to compete with the best champagnes.

The trend to introduce strict quality certifications for food products is more recent but it has gradually extended to a variety of regional specialties, including Parma ham, buffalo mozzarella, and Parmesan cheese. The birth and spread of the Slow Food movement has further promoted the public's appetite for authentic local produce, contributing to a renewed international interest in Italian food. While about 70 per cent of food exports are directed at European countries, Italy has made inroads into the Asian market, especially Thailand, China, and India. Indeed, Thailand is one of the fastest growing importers of Italian food, despite the absence of historical ties or a sizeable Italian minority. The reputation of the Mediterranean diet and of certain brands makes up for these disadvantages, with the result that the popularity of Italian cuisine in Asia seems destined to surpass that of the French.

One area where Italy is still behind its competitors is that of restaurants offering innovative culinary styles. This is partly due to the fact that Italians tend to have conservative tastes and like to follow traditional recipes. Yet a new generation of young chefs have started to redress this situation by using local ingredients and giving well-known dishes a contemporary twist. The region at the forefront of this trend is Piedmont, the same region where a new concept in food and eateries led in 2007 to the opening of the first Eataly outlet, a combination of food market, restaurant, and cooking school, in a disused Vermouth factory close to the Fiat Lingotto plant. Part of the renaissance of Turin following de-industrialization, Eataly is becoming an international phenomenon.

There are obvious tensions between the ideas underpinning the Slow Food movement, especially its crusade against industrially produced food, and the global and aggressive branding of Eataly. These contradictions were replicated at the 2015 Milan Expo exhibition, where the values of food preservation and environmental sustainability were showcased to the public even while business meetings aimed at securing commercial deals were being held and the event was being turned into a lever for furthering international relations. The strategic role played by food in Italy's global image and the 'Made in Italy' brand, as well as in provoking a radical rethinking of waste and poverty in contemporary societies, largely accounts for these tensions. Beyond these divisions, Italians appear to have changed their eating habits following the recent economic crisis. They have gone back to a traditional Mediterranean diet of bread, pasta, and vegetables, cutting down on meat consumption and buying products directly from farmers. The new frugality, however, is not so much due to the growth of ethical consumers as to the increase in the numbers of those who have a limited budget.

Fashion and sport

Italian fashion started to seduce the world in the 1950s, when the first fashion show in Florence aimed at American buyers was a resounding success and Italian haute couture began to rival the dominant French designers. The Fontana sisters and Emilio Pucci were among the first Italian designers to be known internationally, initiating two enduring trends: glamour and luxury on the one hand, and casual elegance on the other. The Fontana sisters were the first to associate themselves with Hollywood stars in the 1950s, a trend which continued in the decade that followed when Italy—and especially Rome—became a favourite destination for American directors and actors, and where Valentino designed clothes for film stars both on and off the screen. Pucci launched an easy to wear yet chic fashion and will remain famous for creating the so-called Capri style, especially summer pants and sandals. Another famous fashion house of those decades, Gucci, specialized in accessories as well as clothing, with silk head scarfs as well as leather and bamboo handbags as its main trademarks.

From the 1970s onwards the centre for Italian fashion shifted from Florence and Rome to Milan where Giorgio Armani and

Gianni Versace became the undisputed leaders of fashion. Armani's understated elegance and Versace's outrageous flamboyance appealed to and catered for different tastes and their fashion houses continue to dress actors and celebrities. Italy's strong reputation in the world of high fashion lasted well into the 1990s, with the affirmation of the Prada and Dolce & Gabbana labels, also based in Milan, and the revival of the Gucci brand. In the 1960s, however, the rise of youth culture and the transition to ready-to-wear clothes posed a challenge to Italian designers. This was met at least in part by the colourful and non-conventional clothes designed by Elio Fiorucci and later by the casual style popularized by the Benetton company. The latter firm rose to international fame in the 1980s also thanks to the controversial advertising campaigns devised by photographer Oliviero Toscani.

In recent years, however, there has been a sense that Italian designers have lost their traditional flair for creativity and innovation. This has been attributed both to the family ownership of many fashion companies and to the inability of their founders to pass the baton to a younger generation more ready to experiment with new styles. As we saw in Chapter 4, this same criticism was raised in relation to Italian industry as a whole. An additional issue relates to the conservative and fairly conventional style of dressing preferred by the vast majority of Italians, which tends to stifle experimentation. Milan is a case in point, as people there are generally elegantly dressed yet they also tend to adopt a fairly uniform style. Starting in the 2010s, however, Italian fashion houses appear to have successfully fought back and defied gloomy predictions. A generational turnover and greater openness to outside investment and influence—the House of Krizia, for instance, was acquired in 2013 by a Chinese female entrepreneur—have led to renewal, and Italian fashion is being hailed for its newly found creativity. Even haute couture is back, with exclusive handmade creations being manufactured using the most expensive materials. Indeed, the renewed appetite for luxury materials such as silk has even convinced some Italian fashion

10. **Celebrations for Italy's world cup win, 2006.**

houses to sponsor the rearing of silkworms on Italian soil, thus re-establishing a tradition that goes back several centuries.

Sport, like fashion, is a crucially important dimension of Italy's soft power. During the fascist period it was also considered an integral part of hard power, as sport was used to promote male virility and military training as well as being viewed as an important instrument of propaganda abroad, demonstrating national prowess and discipline. Furthermore, sporting achievements and leisure facilities helped the regime gain popular consent. In the post-war period Italy's participation in international sporting events, including the hosting of the Olympic Games in 1960 in Rome, helped the country achieve rehabilitation and resume peaceful relations.

Nowadays, sport often acts as an advertisement for the country as a whole, but this can work both ways. When Italian athletes and teams excel in international competitions, the reputation of 'Italy Plc' is enhanced (Figure 10). However, when football, the favourite national game and the one Italy is still best known for, is repeatedly tarnished by widespread corruption and instances of racist behaviour, it quickly becomes a symbol of moral and national decline. This happened for example in 2006 when a major investigation unearthed a match-fixing scandal which resulted in the relegation of one of the country's best known clubs, Juventus. Italian football matches are often marred by racist chants and abuse aimed at both foreign and home players, as repeatedly was the case for striker Mario Balotelli, who is Ghanaian born but grew up in Italy and has citizenship status.

Between fashion and sport there is an obvious crossover. Sportswear represents a highly regarded branch of fashion design. The presence of Italian athletes and teams in almost every sports competition has led companies to launch ever more diversified and specialist collections and the know-how of Italian manufacturers has ensured their primacy at the high end of the market. Even famous international brands like Nike and Puma offer top of the range collections where the high price tag is justified by the assurance that they are 'Made in Italy'—which in turn guarantees premium quality. It is not unusual for fashion companies to enter the world of sport, as Benetton did when it competed in Formula 1 between 1986 and 2001. Conversely, Ferrari has diversified into fashion, as the company offers its own range of sports clothing and accessories. The potential of combining fashion and sport for enhancing the national image abroad was exploited when Dolce & Gabbana dressed the 2012 Italian football team and Armani supplied the outfits for the Italian team at the 2012 London Olympics and the 2014 Sochi winter games, something he agreed to repeat for the 2016 Olympics.

Cultural diplomacy and peacekeeping

Italy has long practised cultural diplomacy as a foreign policy tool. During the fascist period, Italian culture was promoted abroad largely as an instrument of political propaganda, while in the post-war period it was skilfully relied upon to re-establish Italy's credibility among the international community as a democratic country striving for peaceful cooperation. More recently, following the country's economic decline, greater attention has been paid by successive governments to the crucial role exercised by culture for both promoting exports and achieving greater political influence.

Italy's cultural diplomacy and soft power benefit from the prominent role played by its Ministry of Foreign Affairs. This body is especially active in furthering Italian culture and language abroad, with the support of eighty-three cultural institutes, 423 committees of the Società Dante Alighieri, over 300 Italian-teaching schools, and fully-funded language teachers working in over 200 foreign universities. As a result of this concerted effort, in 2014 Italian was the fourth most studied language in the world. The country has a strong cultural presence in Russia and in the former Republics of the USSR, and in recent years it has intensified its cooperation with Asian countries, especially China and Vietnam, where it has opened new consulates and organized cultural activities, in recognition of their growing importance for trade and business.

Although strictly speaking peacekeeping missions cut across 'hard' and 'soft' power, they represent a way of using the military for diplomatic and humanitarian purposes. Italy has embraced participation in international peace operations under the umbrella of the United Nations, as this is both in line with its strategic goals and helps it achieve a positive reputation worldwide. According to Article 11 of the Italian Constitution, 'Italy rejects war as an instrument of aggression against the freedom of other peoples and as a means for the settlement of international disputes'. In addition, Italian public opinion has consistently opposed any war operations. By contrast, humanitarian and peacekeeping intervention is viewed much more favourably, often receiving bipartisan support in Parliament. As the president of the Republic, Sergio Mattarella, stated in 2015, the country was 'committed to the respect of human rights and the search for peace, stability, security, economic and social development ... Even today, the capacity for dialogue and cooperation is the engine of our foreign policy'.

As a result, Italy is one of the major contributors to the UN peacekeeping budget and also one of its top providers in terms of troops committed. Since the early 1980s, when Italy took part in peacekeeping operations in Lebanon, despite some ridiculing of its plumed Bersaglieri troops in the British press, the country's international credibility has been considerably enhanced. In 2007, Italy was asked to head the UN Interim Force in Lebanon (UNIFIL) mission, a role it exercised until 2010 and resumed in 2012. The country's commitment to peacekeeping operations is strengthened by the presence of two important structures on its territory. The United Nations Logistics Base (UNLB) has been based in Brindisi since the mid-1990s and has become a strategic support centre for all UN interventions, while the Centre of Excellence for Stability Police Units (COESPU) was established in 2005 in Vicenza in cooperation with the United States. The latter specializes in training foreign police units in peace operations, largely relying on the special Carabinieri force, which has both military and police responsibilities, and has played a major role in all the peace missions in which Italy has participated. The quality of the training provided at COESPU has been acknowledged by various bodies including the UN.

Finally, as highlighted in Chapter 5, in the 2010s, Italy won international recognition for its rescue operations in the Mediterranean. Leading human rights organizations, including the United Nations High Commissioner for Refugees (UNHCR) and the International Organization for Migration (IOM) as well as Pope Francis, were among those who poured praise on the country's humanitarian interventions. There was also widespread acknowledgment of the disproportionate burden carried by Italy in all patrol and rescue missions at sea.

Renewing Italy's image

Art, culture, fashion, design, food, and sport have all contributed to Italy's seductive, worldwide appeal. While the country was at the forefront of European civilization during the Renaissance and has since built a rich tradition in all these areas, it also witnessed a major artistic explosion in the post-war period. Flair and creativity thrived in a context of industrial development and growing consumerism, yet they also fed upon political dissent, radical experimentation, and youth rebellion. In later decades, Italy was able to rely on its undisputed reputation for sophisticated style and aesthetic excellence, but already by the 1980s continuity appeared to trump innovation. With the advent of globalization, Italy has struggled to regain its prestige at the international level and has had to undergo a process of renewal in almost every branch of productive activity.

Meanwhile successive governments have emphasized the need to promote national excellence through cultural primacy. Each cultural sector is viewed as overlapping with and underpinning the others, while internal domestic cohesion is deemed crucial to ensuring unity of purpose in extending 'soft power' abroad. The embracing of the strategy of so-called 'nation branding' (Anholt 2006) by Italian national leaders, not least by Prime Minister Matteo Renzi, who has built his leadership around a positive story of Italianness, has raised criticisms within the country for running the risk of stifling creativity and reproducing stereotypical images. Such criticisms are understandable but perhaps misplaced, as the concerted efforts of corporate Italy can only magnify cultural vibrancy where it exists, and this will only flourish if new radical forms of expression can freely be developed. In contrast to these controversies, the exercising of diplomacy and peacekeeping to raise Italy's standing within the international community has proved less contentious.

Conclusion

Italy's convoluted and problematic relationship with the concept of modernity and the process of modernization has often resulted in a lack of unitary purpose and has at times descended into violent conflict. Thus the years before and after the First World War saw the country torn between opposing modernizing projects, which ultimately led to the demise of the Liberal regime. In the aftermath of the Second World War, when the country experienced rapid economic expansion and the growth of consumerism, internal divisions and controversies resulted in a fruitful explosion of creativity and inventiveness, albeit marred by political violence. In recent decades the country has been going through another critical historical juncture, when the profound transformation of the domestic political landscape following the collapse of the First Republic in the early 1990s overlapped with the transition to a global economy, increasing flows of migration, and bewildering technological advances.

While there has been no descent into violence, grappling with these epochal changes has again proved divisive, and in the 1990s and 2000s Italy was split between different currents of thought and political projects. On the right, Berlusconi's reassuring story of prosperity for all proved attractive to many, while the leader of the Northern League, Umberto Bossi, gained support in the North by guaranteeing economic wealth and social cohesion through secession from the rest of the country. On the left were all those who opposed these narratives, but they were themselves divided over the direction Italy should take and the stories they should be telling. Then in the 2010s, Prime Minister Matteo Renzi resumed a positive narrative of modernization and growth to be achieved through neo-liberal reforms, amid dissent from various sources.

Some of the disquiet and concerns Italians felt towards the recent changes were addressed in 2015 in a book entitled *Babel. Il disincanto della democrazia* ('Babel. The Disenchantment with Democracy'), written by the philosopher Zygmunt Bauman in collaboration with the journalist Ezio Mauro, editor of the influential newspaper *La Repubblica*. This work attracted much interest and generated considerable public debate. At the book launch in Turin, Mauro dwelt upon the Gramscian concept of the 'interregnum' as characterizing the current historical phase, which he defined as a period 'suspended between that which is no longer and that which is not yet'. Political movements and ideologies seemed unable to articulate the way forward, democratic institutions and the EU appeared to have lost their legitimacy and foreigners were no longer distant but in our midst, requiring constant dialogue and an acceptance of diversity. Mauro's analysis was obviously informed by the Italian case. Indeed his proposed 'solution', in which doubting is seen as the best antidote to 'the seduction exercised by the tangible benefits of modernity', also struck a sceptical chord with many Italians who are unconvinced by any uncritical modernizing narrative.

Beyond internal divisions, controversies, and disagreements, the unity of Italy as a nation-state has been thoroughly tested and has proved to be very resilient. Secessionism is no longer being pursued or being perceived as a credible project. The country's durability recalls a short story published by Goffredo Parise in 1982, entitled *Italia*, in which the main character, Giovanni, has a brief exchange with a Frenchman:

One day, Giovanni said to a French colleague who was worried about the fate of Italy: *'Tout se tient en Italie'* ['Everything holds fast in Italy']

'Yes, but for how long?'

'For ever.'

Brief chronology

1935–6	Italy conquers Ethiopia
1939	Mussolini and Hitler sign the Pact of Steel
1940	Italy declares war on France and Great Britain
1943	The Allies land in Sicily
1943	Mussolini is arrested by order of the king, who nominates a new government headed by General Pietro Badoglio. The new government signs an armistice with the Allies and later declares war on Germany. Mussolini is liberated by the Germans and entrusted by Hitler to set up an Italian social republic
1944	The Allies land at Anzio, near Rome. The Germans assassinate 335 civilians at the Fosse Ardeatine (Rome) in reprisal for a partisan ambush against German soldiers
1945	Italy is liberated. Mussolini is shot dead by partisans
1946	A referendum establishes a republic
1948	A new republican constitution comes into force. The Christian Democracy (DC) Party wins the political elections and governs the country for more than forty years
1949	Italy joins NATO
1957	Italy becomes a founder member of the European Economic Community
1969	A bomb in Milan kills seventeen people and marks the start of a terrorist campaign
1978	Aldo Moro, president of the DC, is kidnapped and assassinated by the Red Brigades
1992	A scandal on systematic corruption and kickbacks unravels Italy's First Republic
1994	Silvio Berlusconi wins the elections and forms his first government at the head of a centre-right coalition
1996	Romano Prodi wins the elections and forms a centre-left government
2014	Matteo Renzi becomes Italy's youngest ever prime minister

References

Introduction

Di Virgilio, Aldo and Radaelli, Claudio M. 'Introduction: The Year of the External Podestà'. In A. Di Virgilio and C. M. Radaelli. eds. *Italian Politics: Technocrats in Office*, 35–57. New York and Oxford: Berghahn, 2013.

On 'amoral familism', see Banfield, Edward C. *The Moral Basis of a Backward Society*. Glencoe, IL: The Free Press, 1958.

Chapter 1: Modernity and resurgence in the making of Italy

Pirandello, Luigi. *I vecchi e i giovani*. 1st edn. Milan: Treves, 1913.

Gladstone, quoted in Deryk M. Schreuder, 'Gladstone and Italian Unification, 1848–70: The Making of a Liberal?' *The English Historical Review*, July 1970, 475–501.

Gramsci, Antonio. *Prison Notebooks*, Volumes 1–3. Columbia University Press, 2011.

Verga, Giovanni. *I Malavoglia*. 1st edn. Milan: Treves, 1881.

Verga, Giovanni. 'La libertà', first published in 1882 in *Domenica letteraria*, and a year later in *Novelle rusticane* (Turin: Casanova, 1883).

Collodi, Carlo. *Le avventure di Pinocchio. Storia di un burattino*. Florence: Felice Paggi Libraio-Editore, 1883.

De Amicis, Edmondo. *Cuore. Libro per i ragazzi*. Milan: Treves, 1886.

Filippo T. Marinetti. 'Manifeste du futurisme'. *Le Figaro*, 20 February 1909 (also published in various Italian newspapers in the same month).

Chapter 2: Alternative projects of nationhood

Ciano, Costanzo. *The Ciano Diaries: The Complete, Unabridged Diaries of Count Galeazzo Ciano, Italian Minister for Foreign Affairs, 1936–1943*, ed. by Hugh Gibson. New York: H. Fertig, 1946.

De Gasperi, Alcide. *La politica europea. Discorso ai giovani*. Rome: Senato della Repubblica, 15 November 1950. <http://www.deputatipd.it/files/documenti/DeGasperiWEB.pdf>.

Hobsbawm, Eric J. and Giorgio Napolitano. *The Italian Road to Socialism: An Interview*. Chicago: Lawrence Hill, 1977.

Cassano, Franco. *Il pensiero meridiano*. Rome-Bari: Laterza, 1996.

Petrini, Carlo, quoted in Peter Popham, 'Carlo Petrini: The Slow Food gourmet who started a revolution'. *The Independent*, 10 December 2009.

Chapter 3: Governing Italy

Sonnino, Sidney. 'Torniamo allo Statuto'. *Nuova Antologia*, 1 January 1897.

Depretis, quoted in Fulvio Cammarano. *Storia dell'Italia liberale*. Rome-Bari: Laterza, 2011, 92.

Minghetti, Marco. *Speech in Parliament*, 12 May 1883. <http://storia.camera.it/regno/lavori/leg15/sed112.pdf>.

King Humbert I, quoted in Antonello Capurso, *Le frasi celebri nella storia d'Italia. Da Vittorio Emanuele II a Silvio Berlusconi*. Milan: Mondadori, 2011.

Fo, Dario. *Morte accidentale di un anarchico*. Milan: La Comune, 1970.

Fabbrini, Sergio. 'The Institutional Odyssey of the Italian Parliamentary Republic'. *Journal of Modern Italian Studies*, 17/1, 2012, 10–24.

Rizzo, Sergio and Gian Antonio Stella. *La casta. Così i politici italiani sono diventati intoccabili*. Milan: Rizzoli, 2007.

Chapter 4: 'Made in Italy'

Nitti, Francesco Saverio. *La conquista della forza. L'elettricità a buon mercato. La nazionalizzazione delle risorse idrauliche*. Turin-Rome: Roux & Viarengo, 1905.

Catani, Sandro. *Gerontocrazia. Il sistema economico che paralizza l'Italia*. Milan: Garzanti, 2014.

Chapter 5: Emigration, immigration, and citizenship

Tremaglia, Mirko. *Speech in Parliament*, 30 June 1999. <http://www.sitocgie.com/index.php/fr/archivio-doc/archivio-1/leggi-1/3188-prop-legge-tremaglia-mod-art-48-c-d-p-luglio-1999/file>.

Mantica, Alfredo, quoted in the newsletter of the Ministry of Cultural Heritage and Activities. <http://www.beniculturali.it/mibac/export/MiBAC/sito-MiBAC/Contenuti/Ministero/UfficioStampa/News/visualizza_asset.html_476563799.html>.

Kyenge, Cécile, quoted in Marina Forti, 'Italy: Ease nationality obstacles for immigrants', *Al Jazeera*, 23 April 2013. <http://www.aljazeera.com/indepth/opinion/2013/04/2013418124142348923.html>.

Chapter 6: Italy's 'soft' power

Eco, Umberto. *Il nome della rosa*. Milan: Bompiani, 1980.

Saviano, Roberto. *Gomorra*. Milan: Mondadori, 2006.

Mayes, Frances. *Under the Tuscan Sun*. New York: Broadway Books, 1996.

Mattarella, Sergio. 'Diplomazia per l'Italia'. Speech delivered at the XI Conference of Italian Ambassadors, 27 July 2015. <http://www.quirinale.it/elementi/Continua.aspx?tipo=Discorso&key=95>.

Anholt, Simon. *Competitive Identity: The New Brand Management for Nations, Cities and Regions*. Basingstoke and New York: Palgrave Macmillan, 2007.

Joseph S. Nye, Jr. *Soft Power: The Means to Success in World Politics*. New York: PublicAffairs, 2004, 15.

Conclusion

Bauman, Zygmunt and Ezio Mauro. *Babel. Il disincanto della democrazia*. Rome-Bari: Laterza, 2015.

Parise, Goffredo. 'Italia'. In *Sillabario n. 2*. Milan: Mondadori, 1982.

Further reading

General

Davis, John A. ed. *Italy in the Nineteenth Century: 1796–1900*.
    Oxford: Oxford University Press, 2000.
Dunnage, Jonathan. *Twentieth Century Italy: A Social History*.
    London: Routledge, 2002.
Gentiloni Silveri U. ed. 'Italy 1980–2014: The Transition that Never
    Happened', Special Issue, *Journal of Modern Italian Studies*, 20/2,
    2015.
Ginsborg, Paul. *A History of Contemporary Italy: Society and Politics,
    1943–1988*. London: Penguin, 1990.
Ginsborg, Paul. *Italy and Its Discontents. Family, Civil Society, State
    1980–2001*. London: Penguin, 2001.
Jones, Erik and Gianfranco Pasquino. *The Oxford Handbook of Italian
    Politics*. Oxford: Oxford University Press, 2015.
Lyttelton, A. ed. *Liberal and Fascist Italy, 1900–1945*. Oxford: Oxford
    University Press, 2002.
Toniolo, G. ed. *The Oxford Handbook of the Italian Economy since
    Unification*. Oxford: Oxford University Press, 2013.

Introduction

Journal of Modern Italian Studies. 'Special Section: Italy on the 150th
    Anniversary of National Unity', 19/1, 2014, 34–77.
Sorrentino, Paolo and Umberto Contarello. *La grande bellezza*. Milan:
    Skira, 2013.

Chapter 1: Modernity and resurgence in the making of Italy

Banti, Alberto Mario. *La nazione del Risorgimento. Parentela, santità e onore alle origini dell'Italia unita.* Turin: Einaudi, 2006.

Ben-Ghiat, Ruth and Mia Fuller. eds. *Italian Colonialism.* Basingstoke and New York: Palgrave Macmillan, 2005.

Duggan, Christopher. *Francesco Crispi 1818-1901: From Nation to Nationalism.* Oxford: Oxford University Press, 2002.

De Grand, Alexander. *The Hunchback's Tailor: Giovanni Giolitti and Liberal Italy from the Challenge of Mass Politics to the Rise of Fascism, 1882-1922.* Westport, CT: Praeger, 2000.

Gentile, Emilio. *The Struggle for Modernity: Nationalism, Futurism, and Fascism.* Westport, CT, and London: Praeger, 2003.

Graziano, Manlio. *The Failure of Italian Nationhood: The Geopolitics of a Troubled Identity.* Basingstoke and New York: Palgrave Macmillan, 2010.

Griffin, Roger. *Modernism and Fascism: The Sense of a Beginning under Mussolini and Hitler.* Basingstoke and London: Palgrave Macmillan, 2007.

Jemolo, Arturo Carlo. *Church and State in Italy, 1850-1960.* Oxford: Blackwell 1960.

Miller, James E. *From Elite to Mass Politics: Italian Socialism in the Giolittian Era, 1900-1914.* Kent, OH, and London: Kent State University Press, 1990.

Patriarca, Silvana. *Italian Vices: Nation and Character from the Risorgimento to the Republic.* Cambridge: Cambridge University Press, 2010.

Pollard, John. *Catholicism in Modern Italy: Religion, Society and Politics since 1861.* London and New York: Routledge, 2008.

Riall, Lucy. *Risorgimento: The History of Italy from Risorgimento to Nation State.* Basingstoke and London: Palgrave Macmillan, 2009.

Schneider, Jane. *Italy's 'Southern Question': Orientalism in One Country.* London: Bloomsbury Academic, 1998.

Chapter 2: Alternative projects of nationhood

Agosti, Aldo. *Palmiro Togliatti: A Biography.* London and New York: I. B. Tauris, 2008.

Ben-Ghiat, Ruth. *Fascist Modernities: Italy, 1922-1945.* Berkeley and Los Angeles: University of California Press, 2004.

Barkan, Joanne. *Visions of Emancipation: the Italian Workers' Movement Since 1945*. New York: Praeger, 1984.

Berezin, Mabel. *Making the Fascist Self: The Political Culture of Interwar Italy*. London: Cornell University Press, 1997.

Corner, Paul. *The Fascist Party and Popular Opinion in Mussolini's Italy*. Oxford: Oxford University Press, 2012.

Craveri, Piero. *De Gasperi*. Bologna: il Mulino, 2006.

De Grazia, Victoria. *How Fascism Ruled Women: Italy, 1922–1945*. Berkeley and Los Angeles: University of California Press, 1993.

Duggan, Christopher. *Fascist Voices: An Intimate History of Mussolini's Italy*. Oxford: Oxford University Press, 2013.

Forgacs, David and Stephen Gundle. *Mass Culture and Italian Society from Fascism to the Cold War*. Bloomington, IN: Indiana University Press, 2007.

Formigoni, Guido. *Alla prova della democrazia. Chiesa, cattolici e modernità nell'Italia del '900*. Trento: Il Margine, 2008.

Ginsborg, Paul. *Silvio Berlusconi. Television, Power and Patrimony*. London: Verso, 2004.

Gundle, Stephen. *Between Hollywood and Moscow: The Italian Communists and the Challenge of Mass Culture, 1943–1991*. Durham and London: Duke University Press, 2000.

Kaiser, Wolfram. *Christian Democracy and the Origins of the European Union*. Cambridge: Cambridge University Press, 2011.

Passerini, Luisa. *Fascism in Popular Memory: The Cultural Experience of the Turin Working Class*. Cambridge: Cambridge University Press, 1987.

Pavone, Claudio. *A Civil War: A History of the Italian Resistance*. London: Verso, 2013.

Pombeni, Paolo. ed. 'De Gasperi's scritti e discorsi politici', *Modern Italy*, 14/4, 2009.

Viroli, Maurizio. *The Liberty of Servants: Berlusconi's Italy*. Princeton: Princeton University Press, 2011.

Chapter 3: Governing Italy

Biorcio, Roberto and Paolo Natale. *Politica a 5 stelle. Idee, storia e strategie del movimento di Grillo*. Milan: Feltrinelli, 2013.

Bull, Martin and Martin Rhodes. *Italy: A Contested Polity*. London: Routledge, 2009.

Cento Bull, Anna and Mark Gilbert. *The Lega Nord and the Northern Question in Italian Politics*. Basingstoke and London: Palgrave MacMillan, 2001.

Cento Bull, Anna and Philip Cooke. *Ending Terrorism in Italy*. London and New York: Routledge, 2013.

Dickie, John. *Mafia Brotherhoods: Camorra, Mafia, 'Ndrangheta'. The Rise of the Honoured Societies*. London: Spectre, 2012.

Duggan, Christopher and Christopher Wagstaff. eds. *Italy in the Cold War: Politics, Culture and Society, 1948–58*. Oxford: Berg, 1995.

Gilbert, Mark. *The End of Politics Italian Style?* Boulder, CO: Westview Press, 1995.

Hine, David. *Governing Italy*. Oxford: Oxford University Press, 1993.

Leonardi, Robert and Douglas A. Wertman. *Italian Christian Democracy: The Politics of Dominance*. Basingstoke and New York: Palgrave Macmillan, 1989.

Musella, Luigi. *Il trasformismo*. Bologna: il Mulino, 2003.

Sabbatucci, Giovanni. *Il trasformismo come sistema*. Rome-Bari: Laterza, 2003.

McCarthy, Patrick. *The Crisis of the Italian State: From the Origins of the Cold War to the Fall of Berlusconi and Beyond*. New York: St Martin's Press, 1995.

Poli, Emanuela. *Forza Italia. Strutture, leadership e radicamento territoriale*. Bologna: il Mulino, 2001.

Sassoon, Donald. *The Strategy of the Italian Communist Party: From the Resistance to the Historic Compromise*. London: Pinter, 1981.

Saviano, Roberto. *Gomorrah: Italy's other Mafia*. Basingstoke and New York: Palgrave Macmillan, 2007.

Chapter 4: 'Made in Italy'

Becattini, Gacomo, Marco Bellandi and Lisa De Propris. eds. *A Handbook of Industrial Districts*. Celtenham and Northampton, MA: Edward Elgar, 2009.

Cohen, John and Giovanni Federico. *The Growth of the Italian Economy 1820–1960*. Cambridge: Cambridge University Press, 2001.

Cento Bull, Anna and Paul Corner. *From Peasant to Entrepreneur: The Survival of the Family Economy in Italy*. London: Berg, 1993.

Di Matteo, Massimo and Paolo Picentini. eds. *The Italian Economy at the Dawn of the 21st Century*. Aldershot: Ashgate, 2003.

Modern Italy

Goodman, Edward, Julia Bamford and Peter Saynor. eds. *Small Firms and Industrial Districts in Italy*. London and New York: Routledge, 1989.

Locke, Richard M. *Remaking the Italian Economy*. Ithaca, NY: Cornell University Press, 1997.

Nanetti, Raffaella. *Growth and Territorial Policies: The Italian Model of Social Capitalism*. London: Pinter, 1988.

Putnam, Robert D., Robert Leonardi, and Raffaella Y. Nanetti. *Making Democracy Work: Civic Traditions in Modern Italy*. Princeton: Princeton University Press, 1993.

Trigilia, Carlo. *Non c'è Nord senza Sud. Perché la crescita dell'Italia si decide nel Mezzogiorno*. Bologna: il Mulino, 2012.

Zamagni, Vera. *The Economic History of Italy 1860–1990*. Oxford: Oxford University Press, 1993.

Chapter 5: Emigration, immigration, and citizenship

Ambrosini, Maurizio. *Richiesti e respinti. L'immigrazione in Italia. Come e perché*. Milan: Il Saggiatore, 2010.

Andall, Jacqueline. *Gender, Migration and Domestic Service: The Politics of Black Women in Italy*. Aldershot: Ashgate, 2000.

Andall, Jacqueline and Derek Duncan. eds. *Italian Colonialism: Legacy and Memory*. Oxford: Peter Lang, 2005.

Choate, Mark I. *Emigrant Nation: The Making of Italy Abroad*. Cambridge, MA, and London: Harvard University Press, 2008.

Choate, Mark I. 'Italy at Home and Abroad After 150 Years: The Legacy of Emigration and the Future of *Italianità*'. In *Italian Culture*, 30/1, 2012, 51–67.

Colombo, Asher and Giuseppe Sciortino. *Gli immigrati in Italia*. Bologna: il Mulino, 2004.

Del Boca, Angelo. *Gli italiani in Africa orientale*. 4 volumes. Bari: Laterza, 1976, 1979, 1982, 1984. Reprinted by Mondadori, Milan, in 1992.

Del Boca, Angelo. *Gli italiani in Libia*. 2 volumes. Bari: Laterza, 1986. Reprinted by Mondadori, Milan, in 1993.

Gabaccia, Donna R. *Italy's Many Diasporas*. Seattle: University of Washington Press, 2000.

Pedote, Paolo and Nicoletta Poidimani. eds. *We will survive! Lesbiche, gay e trans in Italia*. Milano: Mimesis, 2007.

Reeder, L. *Widows in White: Migration and the Transformation of Rural Italian Women, Sicily, 1880–1920*. Toronto, University of Toronto Press, 2003.

Wilson, Perry. *Women in Twentieth-Century Italy*. Basingstoke and New York: Palgrave Macmillan, 2010.

Chapter 6: Italy's 'soft' power

Bondanella, Peter. *A History of Italian Cinema*. New York and London: Continuum, 2009.

Dickie, John. *Delizia! The Epic History of the Italians and their Food*. London: Hodder and Stoughton, 2007.

Filiputti, Walter. *Modern History of Italian Wine*. Milan: Skira, 2016.

Foot, John. *Calcio: A History of Italian Football*. London: Harper Perennial, 2006.

Hainsworth, Peter and David Robey. *Italian Literature: A Very Short Introduction*. Oxford: Oxford University Press, 2012.

Hallamore Caesar, Ann and Michael Caesar. *Modern Italian Literature*. London: Polity, 2007.

Hibberd, Matthew. 'National Tastes: Italy and Food Culture'. In Jeremy Strong, ed., *Educated Tastes: Food, Drink, and Connoisseur Culture*. Lincoln and New York: University of Nebraska Press, 2011.

Kirk, Terry. *The Architecture of Modern Italy. Volume II: Visions of Utopia, 1900–Present*. New York: Princeton Architectural Press, 2005.

Lees-Maffei, Grace and Kjetil Fallan. eds. *Made in Italy: Rethinking a Century of Italian Design*. London and New York: Bloomsbury, 2014.

Lupano, Mario and Alessandra Vaccari. *Fashion at the Time of Fascism: Italian Modernist Lifestyle, 1922–1943*. Bologna: Damiani, 2009.

Mariani, John F. *How Italian Food Conquered the World*. Basingstoke and New York: Palgrave Macmillan, 2011.

Martin, Simon. *Sport Italia: The Italian Love Affair with Sport*. London and New York: I.B. Tauris, 2011.

Rinaldi, Lucia. *Andrea Camilleri: A Companion to the Mystery Fiction*. Jefferson, NC: McFarland, 2012.

Scarpellini, Emanuela. *L'Italia dei consumi. Dalla Belle Époque al nuovo millennio*. Rome-Bari: Laterza, 2008.

Steele, Valeria. *Fashion, Italian Style*. New Haven and London: Yale University Press, 2003.

White, Nicola. *Reconstructing Italian Fashion: America and the Development of the Italian Fashion Industry*. London and New York: Bloomsbury, 2000.

Index

ITALIAN LITERATURE
A Very Short Introduction
Peter Hainsworth and David Robey

In this Very Short Introduction, Peter Hainsworth and David Robey consider Italian literature from the Middle Ages to the present day, looking at themes and issues which have recurred throughout its history and continue to be of importance today.

Examining themes such as regional identities, political disunity, and the role of the national language, they also cover a wide range of authors and works, including Dante, Petrarch, Manzoni, Montale, and Calvino. They explore some of the distinctive traditions of the literature, such as its liking for theorizing its own position, its concern with politics, and its secular orientation in spite of the Catholic beliefs and practices of the Italian people. Concluding by looking at the ways in which Italian literature has changed over the last thirty years, they examine the influence of women's writing in Italian, and acknowledge the belated recognition of its importance.

http://www.oup.co.uk/isbn/9780199231799

SOCIAL MEDIA
Very Short Introduction

Join our community
www.oup.com/vsi

- Join us online at the official Very Short Introductions
  Facebook page.
- Access the thoughts and musings of our authors with our
  online **blog**.
- Sign up for our monthly **e-newsletter** to receive information
  on all new titles publishing that month.
- Browse the full range of Very Short Introductions online.
- Read **extracts** from the Introductions for free.
- If you are a teacher or lecturer you can order inspection
  copies quickly and simply via our website.